TABLE OF CON

BOOK 1
100 Incredible Facts for Curious Children

WE ARE LINDA AND CHARLIE,
FOUNDERS OF KAIROSLANDD **9**

INTRODUCTION **11**

**CURIOSITIES ABOUT
GEOGRAPHY AND TOURISM**
THE MOST IMPROBABLE FACTS
WHEN TRAVELING AROUND
THE PLANET **12**

SCIENTIFIC CURIOSITIES
FACTS ABOUT SCIENCE AND
TECHNOLOGY THAT YOU MAY
HAVE NEVER HEARD BEFORE . **19**

CURIOSITIES ABOUT FEEDING
 FUN REVELATIONS ABOUT
FOOD **26**

**ANTHROPOLOGICAL
CURIOSITIES**
CUSTOMS AND PECULIARITIES
OF PEOPLES WHOSE
EXISTENCE YOU MAY BE
UNAWARE OF **33**

CURIOSITIES OF NATURE
THE MOST UNLIKELY FACTS
OF THE ANIMAL AND PLANT
KINGDOMS **38**

CURIOSITIES ABOUT HISTORY
HISTORICAL FACTS YOU MIGHT
NOT KNOW! **45**

CURIOSITIES ABOUT CINEMA
FROM HOLLYWOOD TO
HOGWARTS AND THROUGH
SPACE **59**

NIGHTMARISH CURIOSITIES
THE MOST UNLIKELY PHOBIAS **64**

**CURIOSITIES ABOUT THE
HUMAN BODY**
BETWEEN TRINKETS AND
SUPERPOWERS!..................... **71**

CONCLUSION **77**

GLOSSARY **78**

THE FINAL TRIVIA QUIZ **79**

SOLUTIONS **82**

BOOK 2
Astonishing Inventions for Curious Kids

INTRODUCTION...................**84**

FOOD. SO MANY SURPRISING DELIGHTS!...................**87**

SCHOOL: FROM CLAY TABLETS TO CALCULATORS...................**92**

GAMES AND LEISURE. DO YOU REMEMBER PLAYING WITH THE PONGO?...................**102**

TECHNOLOGY. INNOVATIONS AS A WINDOW TO THE WORLD **109**

ORDINARY OBJECTS. THEY'RE NOT SO OBVIOUS! **116**

CONCLUSIONS **127**

QUIZ **129**

BIBLIOGRAPHY **132**

KAIROSLANDD **133**

SPECIAL QR BONUS **134**

ANSWERS **135**

BOOK 1

100 INCREDIBLE FACTS FOR CURIOUS CHILDREN

WE ARE LINDA AND CHARLIE, FOUNDERS OF KAIROSLANDD

Firstly, we would like to thank you for your purchase and most importantly for trusting us. As a token of our appreciation, we offer you a SPECIAL BONUS to keep having fun and laughter, alone or with your friends. Discover what awaits you on the back cover and.share your thoughts with us!

9

INTRODUCTION

Dear smart boys and girls of all ages, are you ready for a fun and rewarding journey filled with news, discoveries, incredible facts to satisfy your curiosity, and perhaps impress your friends? Turn off the TV and video games, and get ready to read articles about the weirdest, funniest, and strangest things from all corners of the planet.

We will talk about bizarre food, incredible facts about history and science, curiosities of the animal world and nature, populations, the most improbable records, sports, inventions, science, terrifying fears, proverbs, as well as thought-provoking elements that will keep you and your family on the edge of your seats.

At the end of the book, you will find a glossary where you can discover the meaning of the most complicated terms. You will find them in **BOLD** and <u>UNDERLINED</u> in the text. And that's not all! In fact, at the end of your reading, you will also find a game to test your new knowledge: the "Final Quiz of Curiosities!"

That's right! After reading all these incredible and sensational stories, test yourself by trying to answer the questions correctly and even challenging your parents, siblings, or classmates.

Whoever gets the most correct answers wins.

READY TO TAKE ON THE CHALLENGE?

Happy reading to all.

Curiosities About Geography and Tourism

THE MOST IMPROBABLE FACTS WHEN TRAVELING AROUND THE PLANET

THE CRAZIEST LAWS IN AMERICA!

In every state, the law, even the most insane, applies to everyone and must always be respected. However, you should know that there are regulations in the world that are so bizarre and incredible that you will wonder how it was possible to adopt them. At first glance, many of them not only seem useless but also ridiculous and senseless. The most extravagant, however, is in the United States, where everything (even the creation of laws!) is done in the most spectacular way possible, much like in Hollywood movies. Let's list some of the most absurd ones.

Did you know, for example, that in New York, it is illegal to put an ice cream cone in your pocket on a Sunday while walking on the city streets? Or that in Tryon, North Carolina, you cannot keep a singing bird or play a flute in your house between 11 a.m. and 7 a.m. the following morning? Yes, but the strangeness does not stop there! In Ohio, it is forbidden to serve drinks to fish. In Oklahoma, dogs that want to gather in groups can only do so with the mayor's permission. In Pennsylvania, singing in the bathtub is prohibited. Finally, in Utah, it is illegal to fish sitting on a horse!

THE CITY WITH THE LONGEST NAME IN THE WORLD!

The Guinness Book of Records lists the city with the longest name in the world! The record was initially attributed to a village in Wales whose name had 51 letters, making it a destination for tourists and curious people. The record was later attributed to a hill in New Zealand whose name had 85 letters. But what if I told you that the longest city name has no less than 163 letters? That's right, if you plan to visit this city in Thailand, start by practicing saying its name:

Krung - thep - maha- nakorn - boworn - ratana - kosin - mahintar - ayudhya - amaha - dilok - pop - nopa - ratana - rajthani - burirom - udom - rajniwes - mahasat - arn - amorn - pimarn - avatar - satit - sakattiya -visanukam.

This seems almost impossible, even for the Thai themselves, who decided to shorten the name to Krung Thep. While we're at it, do you want to know what the city with the shortest name in the world is called? It's called "Å", which means "river" and is located in Sweden.

DO YOU WANT TO TAKE A SHOWER?

What question do you get asked every time you are invited to someone's house? If you're in Brazil, you'll be asked if you want to take a shower! It seems to be the first question Brazilians ask you if you are their guest. It would never occur to us to ask this of someone visiting us at home, especially because it seems embarrassing or even perhaps offensive. However, in Brazil, it is customary to offer a shower to any guest who visits you, even if they will not be staying overnight. Indeed, Brazil is a hot country and Brazilians (who are very clean) tend to wash themselves at least two or three times a day. So, rest assured, if a Brazilian asks you this question, they are not insinuating that you smell bad!

THE NEAREST MOUNTAIN TO THE MOON IS NOT THE HIGHEST IN THE WORLD!

WHAT IS THE HIGHEST MOUNTAIN IN THE WORLD?

Easy, it's Mount Everest! Located in the Himalayas, on the border between Nepal and China, it is the highest peak on the planet, reaching 29,029 feet. At this point, you might think that being the highest mountain of all, it is also the closest to the Moon. Not so! The closest summit to the Moon is in Ecuador, it is the Chimborazo volcano, and it is actually lower than Everest! How is this possible? Well, even though it only reaches an altitude of 20,541 feet, this volcano has the advantage of being above the equator! Compared to Everest, it has a few extra kilometers that bring it closer to the Moon.

II DIFFERENT TIME ZONES!

Do you think it's possible to have day and night at the same time? It may sound absurd, but that's the way it is in Russia. How is that possible? Simply because Russia is an immense country. In fact, from west to east, it's so vast (we're talking about 6,601,668 square miles) that it covers no less than 11 different time zones. What does that mean? It means that when the clock in Moscow shows 1:00 pm, in Kamchatka (which is on the opposite side of Russia going east), it's already midnight of the next day. The fact that Russia is the country with the largest number of time zones in the world is not really easy to manage. Indeed, this peculiarity can be a real problem for telecommunications, transportation, and commercial activities. In short, anyone traveling to Russia could seriously be "baffled"!

WHO TRAVELS THE MOST IN THE WORLD?

Which country has the most travelers in the world? Most people would likely answer China or Japan. Although Chinese tourists account for the largest number of international trips (over 97 million recorded in 2013), as a nation, the Chinese do not travel much, and the only reason the number of trips is so high is because of China's size and large population. So, if China does not hold this record, what is the country with the most travelers in the world? It seems to be actually the residents of Scandinavia. And in first place, the Finns with an average of 8 trips per person per year (2 out of 8 trips are international). In second place, we find American tourists with 7 trips per year. Then come Swedish, Danish, and Norwegian travelers (with 5 or 6 trips per year).

THE LONGEST CYCLING TRAIL IN THE WORLD!

If you enjoy cycling in the wild and want to spend a school year in a country that will allow you to fully live your passion, Canada is undoubtedly your dream destination. This is where the longest bike path in the world was inaugurated (we are talking about 1722 miles of uninterrupted road, car-free road). This path crosses incredible and spectacular landscapes, a long road that connects 15,000 Canadian cities and passes through lakes, mountains, famous cities like Vancouver and Montreal, but also remote and pristine areas. The Canadian bike path is significant as it reveals the greatness of Canada with its vastness and the diversity of its sceneries and inhabitants. The project began in 1992, and to carry it out, the Canadian government made available disused and out-of-service railway lines, which were then renovated and converted.

THE MOST VISITED COUNTRY IN THE WORLD!

Do you know which country is the most visited on the planet? According to a ranking by the World Tourism Organization, it seems to be France. Over 80 million tourists visit France every year, including 15 million in the capital city of Paris alone, while the rest go to small villages, to the seaside, to the countryside and to the gastronomy and wine routes. One of the favorite destinations for tourists is the island of Mont Saint Michel, famous for its spectacular tides. After France, the other most visited countries are Spain in second place, the United States in third, China in fourth, and Italy in fifth. If France is the most visited country, Paris does not occupy the first place in terms of tourist influx. In fact, at the top of the list is Hong Kong, which has held the record since 2016 thanks to its incredible economic and cultural growth.

THE SCORPION IS A DELICACY!

You would never have placed any bets on it, but you should know that scorpion is very popular in street food in some countries. Indeed, it is very common to find it on food stalls in the form of tasty kebabs. Of course, these are farmed **scorpions** that are specially selected to be cooked and eaten. This delicious dish is also reported to have benefits for the body.

THE ATACAMA DESERT HASN'T SEEN RAIN FOR 400 YEARS!

Do you know where the driest place on Earth is? In South America, in Chile, you'll find the Atacama Desert: nearly 1,243 miles long and 112 miles wide, it is famous for being one of the driest coastal deserts on the planet. It is said that it has not rained here for more than 400 years!

The geographical position of this desert, closed to the east by the Andes Mountains and to the west by the Coastal Range, means that precipitation is very low.

The area is characterized by a large thermal amplitude, with temperatures oscillating between 41°F at night and 104 °F during the day. In recent years, the Atacama Desert has been used by NASA to conduct experiments and tests for future missions to the planet Mars. Additionally, many science fiction films have been shot there.

FACTS ABOUT SCIENCE AND TECHNOLOGY THAT YOU MAY HAVE NEVER HEARD BEFORE

DO DINOSAURS STILL EXIST?

When it comes to dinosaurs, we imagine huge and fierce reptiles belonging to a bygone era. They appeared on Earth about 230 million years ago and dominated the animal kingdom until a major catastrophic event led to their ultimate extinction. However, paleontologists argue that dinosaurs did

not disappear. Apparently, there are still 10,000 different species alive today, in the form of birds. Some British researchers claim that birds are the only group of dinosaurs that survived the extinction and continued to evolve over time. Unlike the large dinosaurs, these small specimens managed to stay alive, find food, and adapt to environmental and climatic changes. Modern birds are therefore fully-fledged living dinosaurs, so think about that next time you stare at a pigeon!

THE FIRST ROBOT IN HISTORY WAS ITALIAN!

Did you know that the first robot in history was invented in 1500 and that it was Italian? Recognized universally as an absolute genius, both as a painter and inventor, Leonardo da Vinci seems to have conducted extensive research on anatomy, which inspired him to create a "robot" knight. In 1950, researchers set out to build Leonardo's robot, faithfully following the instructions that the Renaissance artist had jotted down on his papers. The result was extraordinary: the built robot worked perfectly! It was a soldier wearing medieval armor capable of standing up, moving its arms, and turning its head. The robot's movements were made possible by ropes, straps, and pulleys. To build today's robots, many scientists continue to draw inspiration from Leonardo da Vinci's designs, who is rightly considered the father of robotics!

DO YOU WANT TO KNOW WHERE FIREWORKS COME FROM?

Many people may know that fireworks began in the East, almost certainly in China, following the invention of gunpowder. But few of you know that these explosions started in a kitchen! Pay close attention to this curious story. About 2,000 years ago, a cook eager to prepare a tasty dish accidentally mixed sulfur, charcoal, and potassium nitrate, ingredients that are easily found in an ordinary kitchen. Potassium nitrate, by the way, is also known as saltpeter and was often used to preserve food in the past. When the cook heated and mixed the three ingredients, a crazy explosion came out of it! The substance created was essentially what we commonly call gunpowder today. It seems that the cook had introduced this mixture inside a bamboo cane, so the bang must have been very loud! The next time you marvel at a fireworks display, remember that its discovery was completely accidental.

THE HIGHEST HOTSPOT IN THE WORLD!

We have all had the experience of trying to call or send a text message to a friend only to find that our smartphone lacks a network. Or you may have noticed that the connection can easily be lost when you are in remote and isolated places. But what if I told you that on Mount Everest, the reception is excellent, would you believe it? Well, it's absolutely true. At 17,585 feet above sea level, the Everest base camp is the highest <u>HOTSPOT</u> on the planet. Indeed, it exists for a specific reason: climbers come here every year to climb mountains, and a good number of them encounter serious difficulties. That is why it was decided to offer a connection system that would facilitate communication in difficult and dangerous situations.

Imagination

21

DO YOU REALLY KNOW EVERYTHING ABOUT SPACESUITS?

You've probably already seen an astronaut in a photo or on TV. Have you noticed that the suits they usually wear are always white? This choice was made because white protects against the sun's cancer-causing radiation. In fact, this color is capable of reflecting most of the sun's rays. These suits are also very comfortable and allow astronauts to walk in space and move freely. However, it is important to know that once back on Earth, due to the force of gravity, a spacesuit weighs a whopping 280 lbs! So, it is not a very light garment as it is in orbit. In space, in fact, without the force of gravity, it weighs absolutely nothing. Additionally, as you know, a spacesuit is also equipped with a space helmet for survival. And how does an astronaut scratch their nose if it itches? Scientists thought of this by inserting a small piece of <u>Velcro</u> inside the helmet. The astronaut just has to rub their nose against the Velcro to relieve the itch.

THE SOUND OF THE SEA!

How many of you have tried to hear the sound of the sea by holding a seashell up to your ear? Have you ever wondered why this curious phenomenon occurs? In reality, what you hear is not really the sound of the sea, but an acoustic illusion. When the sound waves of the environment brush against it, they cause the air inside the shell to vibrate. In this way, even sounds and noises that would normally be inaudible are significantly amplified. The air inside the shell and the external sounds float, while the walls of the shell act as a kind of resonance chamber. That is why, when we hold seashells up to our ears, it seems to us that we can hear the <u>backwash</u> of the sea.

22

DO FLIES ONLY LIVE FOR 24 HOURS?

If you try to ask around how long a fly lives, most people will likely tell you: only 24 hours! Apparently, that's not the case, at least not for all flies! House flies and larger-than-normal flies can actually live for days, even months. If flies live indoors or in warm environments, they can develop quickly and live longer than normal flies. Thus, while a simple fly may indeed live only 24 hours, a housefly can easily live between 20 and 25 days. The life cycle of flies has 4 phases: first the eggs, then the larvae, then the pupae, and finally the adult flies. If a certain number of eggs survive, you may find your home full of flies. If nothing is done, the short life cycle allows these insects to reproduce and multiply quickly. Some house flies are also particularly dangerous, as they are carriers of over 100 diseases!

THE FIRST VIDEO GAME IN HISTORY!

Do you know when the first video game in history was produced and what it was called? It's a very interesting curiosity, and to find the answer, we have to travel back in time, specifically to 1952 in Cambridge, England. Before he knew it, university student Alexander S. Douglas invented OXO, the first video game, a screen adaptation of tic-tac-toe, a game in which you win by aligning 3 circles or 3 Xs on a grid of 9 squares. However, the main objective of OXO was not at all to entertain and have fun playing! It was indeed Douglas' university thesis. EDSAC, one of the first computers in history, which was the size of an entire room, was used for software development! It wasn't until 1961 that the first real video game created for entertainment was released, when a group of young American academics created "Spacewar", a kind of battle between spaceships, considered one of the most popular games of all time.

FOOD ON THE FLOOR!

Do you believe that if food falls on the floor but is picked up within 5 seconds, it's still safe to eat? Some experts say yes, but others are not so sure. Let's try to get to the bottom of this. An American engineer from NASA stated some time ago that it takes 5 seconds for microbes to contaminate food. However, this rule would only apply to certain types of food. The engineer advises against picking up wet food once it is dropped on the ground, as some bacteria like salmonella or Escherichia coli prefer moist environments where they can multiply rapidly, as opposed to dry environments. On the other hand, if food falls on a dry surface, it remains edible if picked up within 5 seconds. However, other researchers claim that food in contact with the ground can be contaminated by microbes in less than a second. The 5-second rule is therefore not always to be taken literally. This is why several doctors strongly advise against eating food that has fallen on the floor.

HEIGHT ALSO CHANGES WITH THE TIME OF THE DAY!

Did you know that after we wake up in the morning and get out of bed, we don't remain the same quite the same for the rest of the day? It turns out that our height, even in a very slight way, varies depending on the time of day. It's possible that upon waking up, we're one or two centimeters taller than we usually are. When we stand upright during the day, the cartilage between the vertebrae in our bones narrows, as it is crushed by the weight of our body. This makes us shorter. But when we sleep, our stretched and relaxed position corrects this compression of the cartilage, so we may be taller by the time we get out of bed!

CRYING IS GOOD FOR YOU!

Crying is a feeling that occurs to all of us. We cry when we're sad, but also when we're happy and particularly moved. Yet, crying is not only a way to express and communicate our mood to others, it's also a psychophysiological function: when we cry, tears promote the release of corticotrophin, the stress hormone. A liberating cry thus seems to help our body slowly return to a state of normalcy and calm, reducing the reaction of high agitation and stress. Other studies also suggest that crying helps with better sleep, fighting bacteria, and improving eyesight.

Curiosities about feeding

FUN REVELATIONS ABOUT FOOD

WHY DOES CHOCOLATE GIVE YOU ENERGY?

You've probably heard these words before: "Eat chocolate! You'll feel better!" If you're a fan of Harry Potter, you'll also remember Professor Remus J. Lupin offering Harry some after he was attacked by a demon. But why do people say that chocolate gives you energy? It turns out that this delicious food is actually the most theobromine-rich substance in nature. <u>Theobromine</u> has a stimulating effect very similar to that of the caffeine found in coffee. Theobromine and caffeine will make you feel more energetic after consuming them. Both act on our brain, specifically on the central nervous system. Eating chocolate therefore stimulates the brain! But be careful not to swallow too much! Like coffee, chocolate, when consumed in large quantities, can lead to side effects such as anxiety and restlessness.

Another thing you probably didn't know is that if you're a true chocolate lover, you should thank the flies. It's true. Very often, these little buzzing insects are seen in a bad light. Many flies are dirty, annoying, and said to spread germs and bacteria. However, in nature, there are flies that belong to the dipteran family (class of insects), which includes more than 110,000 species. Some of them play a very special role, and those with a sweet tooth should be grateful to them. Flies are actually the pollinators of many plants, including the cacao plant, from which chocolate is made. As you can tell, these small and often annoying insects, despite their bad reputation, play a very important role for nature and its fruits.

CROISSANTS ARE NOT REALLY FRENCH!

Are croissants good? You've probably enjoyed them at least once for breakfast, maybe with a cup of cappuccino. But **WHERE DO THEY COME FROM?** Although the name is a French term (literally meaning "crescent" and referring to the shape of a crescent moon), the croissant is not French but was only imported to France in the first half of the 1800s. This cake actually comes from another country: Austria. It is in fact inspired by the Austrian kipferl (or kifli), which was a half-moon shaped pastry, sweet or savory, made of flour, water, eggs, sugar, and butter. Its surface was brushed with egg yolk to make it golden and crispy when baked, just as is still done today with croissants. It was August Zang, an Austrian artillery officer, who imported this pastry to Paris by founding the "BOULANGERIE VIENNOISE" in the early 19th century.

PEANUTS ARE NOT ACTUALLY PEANUTS!

When we talk about peanuts, we instantly associate them with the salty "peanuts" that are often found in appetizers or at birthday parties, or to snack on while watching TV.

However, these "peanuts" are not part of the "nuts" family at all. Peanuts belong to the Leguminosae class (legumes). You probably know other foods that belong to this class, such as beans, peas, and lentils. Another truly amazing fact about peanuts is the delicious butter made by grinding these unique legumes: peanut butter.

You may not have known this, but an Edinburgh professor, Malcolm McMahon, demonstrated something quite bizarre and miraculous using this very tasty snack. It seems that peanut butter is very suitable for transforming into diamonds. On a scientific level, the professor showed that by crushing peanut butter under 5 million atmospheres, the high pressure would actually generate diamonds. However, although the experiment was successful, it only produced very small gems; furthermore, given the high cost of the experiment, it was worth more than the diamond itself. Nonetheless, it remains a unique and sensational discovery!

CHEWING GUM MAKES YOU CRAVE HIGH-CALORIE FOODS

A scientific survey conducted at Ohio State University on 44 volunteers reveals a particular and interesting result about chewing gum. As explained by Christine Swoboda, co-author of the study, chewing gum reduces cravings for healthy foods such as fruits and vegetables. According to this research, mint-flavored chewing gum contains a chemical that alters the taste of vegetables and fruits. In fact, if we consume them immediately after mint-flavored chewing gum, these foods will taste extremely salty and generally unpleasant. Conversely, chewing gum stimulates people to prefer high-calorie and sweeter foods. The same principle applies to peppermint toothpaste. Try brushing your teeth and drinking orange juice immediately after. The special "minty" substance in the toothpaste will make your juice sour, a little salty, and overall, extremely unpleasant. You won't feel like tasting real orange juice anymore!

WHY ARE THERE HOLES IN CRACKERS?

Who doesn't know about crackers? They often make for a quick and convenient snack if we're on the go and need something to munch on to quench our hunger. But have you ever wondered why these salty biscuits usually have holes in them? These holes were added to prevent the formation of air bubbles during baking. Water vapor escapes through these holes, so the cracker retains its flat and thin shape instead of puffing up like a cookie. Finally, those little holes you see on your crackers also help them maintain a crispy texture. You can also change the number of holes and their position on the biscuit. When the holes are far apart, small air bubbles form on the cracker, but if they are too close together, the crackers will appear dry and hard because too much water vapor will have escaped.

WHAT'S IN YOUR FAST-FOOD BURGER?

Did you know that there can be over 100 different kinds of beef in your hamburger bun? McDonald's, a major fast-food chain, admits to this. In fact, the meat in your hamburger does not come from just one cow, but from a combination of meats from at least one hundred different animals. Mc-

Donald's claims that its meat comes from 16,000 different local farmers and is 100% beef in every case. The protocol is to blend the meat from all batches, so the meat from over a hundred different cows can go into the same hamburger. However, as a safety measure, each piece of meat is traced: even if it is mixed, it is possible to trace it back to its batch and its breeder. There are consumer associations that disagree with this view. For them, even though it is possible to trace back to the original batches, the fact that they number in the hundreds makes it extremely difficult and complicated to quickly solve any potential health concern.

THE "SURPRISE PIE": ENGLISH CAKE WITH A SURPRISE!

Without a cake, it's not a real party! However, in the 16th century England, they used to make truly "surprising" pies. Take for example the surprise pie! This particular pie contained an unusual surprise: a live animal! In fact, when you cut into it, it wasn't your dream girl or your favorite singer who came out... but most likely a bird or another screaming animal! This was a typical custom of the English bourgeoisie. Nowadays, surprise pies are still made, but instead of live animals, people prefer more pleasant surprises like a delicious filling!

THE MOST STOLEN FOOD IN THE WORLD!

Perhaps many of you would turn to junk food: candy, pizza, meat or snacks! And yet, listen carefully, it's cheese that is the most stolen food in the world! This curious statistic is reported by the Centre for Retail Research, which designates cheese as the favorite target of supermarket thieves. According to this statistic, thousands of dollars' worth of cheese has already been stolen. For example, a record theft was reported in England, at the Yeovil Show in Somerset. Here, two cheese wheels with a total value of $2,000 were awarded as prizes. Unfortunately, both had been stolen shortly before the event. The owner even placed an ad with a reward to find them, but to no avail. Another record-breaking theft took place at a Wisconsin warehouse. Cheese thieves made off with products worth a staggering $160,000! Unfortunately, these often-excellent products are then sold on the black market, undermining the quality and brand. One of the cheeses most targeted by these thieves is precisely our Parmesan cheese. Very often stolen or counterfeited by unscrupulous people!

WHO INVENTED THE FIRST SANDWICH?

Did you know that sandwiches were invented by a gambler? We are in Great Britain in the first half of the 18th century. Most likely, our inventor was an earl, the "Earl of Sandwich". The nobleman, an inveterate gambler, could not get up from the table to prepare his own food, so he invented the famous stuffed sandwich that we know today. Others claim that the earl was a hard worker, always at his desk with his paperwork, and an avid golfer and card player. Due to his busy schedule, it was difficult for him to stop for lunch, so he made the first sandwich. The snack then spread around the world. In Italian, this sandwich is called "tramezzino". We owe this name to the poet Gabriele D'Annunzio. He thought of calling it tramezzino (from "tra mezzo"), which means something to eat between two moments. In fact, the sandwich is still popular today as a snack during breaks. In 1925, the first "Italian tramezzino" was served at the Mulassano café in Italy. The bread was served in triangular slices, without crust.

PEPPER AS A LUXURY PRODUCT

Here's a curious fact about a spice we all know very well: black pepper. It should be known that in the Middle Ages, these small dark grains were considered in every respect a "luxury product". They were so valuable that with pepper grains, one could pay for very important things like rent or taxes.

CUSTOMS AND PECULIARITIES OF PEOPLES WHOSE EXISTENCE YOU MAY BE UNAWARE OF

CUIVAS DON'T SUFFER FROM STRESS!

Most of us always complain about tending to spend too much time working and always rushing to get everything done. We would like to find more time to relax with our friends and spend more time with our family. Did you know that there are people who work much less than we do? Well, yes! In Venezuela and Colombia, there is a tribe called the Cuiva. They work very few hours in a week (on average between 15 and 20 hours total) to get what they need. It is precisely for this reason that they have much more time to enjoy their leisure days and spend enjoyable hours together in huge hammocks.

LEAVE SOME HONEY FOR THE TIGER!

Many indigenous peoples around the world have an incredible and unparalleled knowledge of certain animals and are capable of maintaining unique and surprising relationships with them. In India, for example, members of the Soliga tribe, when harvesting honey from high branches of trees, do not take it all for themselves. In fact, a portion is left on the ground to be shared with tigers. Why is honey also left for the tigers? Because the Soliga know that these animals have difficulty climbing trees, but also because they consider tigers to be family members.

THE IMPORTANCE OF SHARING

In Africa, more precisely in Tanzania, live the Hadza, a small and very particular tribe. Apparently, they have no religious rituals, no official chiefs or leaders, they do not celebrate birthdays and they do not count the passing of time. Besides these differences that may seem strange to you, the Hadza place great importance to the values of equality and generosity. For them, giving what you have without expecting anything in return is considered a kind of moral obligation, and if you possess more goods than you need, you must always share them with others.

THE TREE OF BIRTH

In Indonesia, on the island of Sumatra, lives the indigenous people of Orang Rimba, which in Bahasa language means "people of the forest". Every time a child is born, their umbilical cord is buried in the ground and a tree is planted in that spot. In this way, the child establishes a deep and sacred bond with that tree that will last their entire life. Every member of the Orang Rimba community is required to defend and protect their tree from being cut down or falling. If that tree is cut down, it would be considered a murder!

THE THOUSAND
USES OF PLANTS

The Yanomami, indigenous people of South America, are considered experts in botany. They use about 500 different types of plants every day for various purposes: for example, building houses or making weapons like arrows. The Yanomami also recognize the most appropriate plants to make fuel, ropes to anchor boats, hammocks or supports. They even use some plants for coloring or painting their faces, or as medicine, poisons, perfumes, and others. Another curiosity of the Yanomami relates to hunting: it seems that they never eat the prey they catch but offer it to others. They eat all animals hunted by others, in order to strengthen the sense of sharing and the spirit of their community.

NEVER "SCRATCH"
MOTHER EARTH!

The Indian tribe of Baiga (which means "sorcerer-medicine man") is famous for its tattoos, its close relationship with the surrounding nature, but above all because it inspired "The Jungle Book", Rudyard Kipling's famous novel. This population believes that plowing a cultivated field is an offense to Mother Earth because it is like scratching her. The Baiga believe that their God created nature and the forest to give man everything he needs. Therefore, it is up to man to deploy his intelligence and wisdom to find what he needs without resorting to agriculture. For the Baiga, only unreasonable people must farm to survive.

NATURE IS THE BEST TECHNOLOGY!

Over the centuries, indigenous peoples have developed incredible skills and unique technologies, not only to survive in the harshest environments on the planet, but also to live longer and in harmony with nature. In Malaysia, the Penan people have developed an absolutely ingenious technique for sustainable fishing without harming the environment, but most importantly, without using a fishing rods and hooks. In fact, the Penan use <u>TOXINS</u> extracted from specific plants to stun and paralyze fish, and once they float to the surface, fishermen only catch the larger ones, while the smaller ones can recover after a few minutes and swim away. This way, fish stocks are never endangered.

A KILLER HAIRCUT!

Did you know that not all hairdressers use scissors and combs to cut hair? In fact, Colombia is home to the Nukak people, who have always used very unusual and bizarre tools to create new hairstyles. It seems that at least until 1988 (the year when this uncontacted tribe decided to leave the forest and make themselves known to the outside world), piranha teeth were traditionally used to cut hair! Absurd, isn't it? They must have had some really wild haircuts!

"MEN IN WIGS"!

We're in the Tari Highlands of Papua New Guinea, where there's a tribe nicknamed the "wig men." This is the Huli tribe, which counts approximately 140 000 souls. Eccentric "wigs" adorn the hats of its male members but are actually made from their own hair! Another custom of this tribe is to wear a leaf skirt, a braid belt, and a claw axe. Members also paint their faces yellow to intimidate rival clans. An animal that is very important to Papua New Guinea, so important that it also appears on the national flag, is the bird of paradise. In honor of this bird, the Huli perform a dance that mimics its movements. This tribe has preserved its ancient traditions, but has also opened up to tourists and outsiders, managing to reconcile its past with modern life.

THE SKELETON DANCE!

Here's another unique tribe from Papua New Guinea, more precisely from the province of Chimbu. They are the " dancing skeletons" of Chimbu. Indeed, its members paint their bodies black like real skeletons, both front and back. The "dancing skeletons" are named after a curious dance that this tribe has been performing since ancient times to scare off their enemies. They come from a very ancient lineage, and little is known about their life to this day. It is certain that they live in the mountains up to 7,874 feet above sea level. Another peculiarity of the group is that in their homes, men and women live separately from each other while keeping their families together. Gradually, the tribe is also opening up to visitors, and it is not uncommon for its members to perform the ancient and evocative "skeleton dance" as a spectacle. This is made possible through mediators who are well-integrated within the tribe.

THE MOST UNLIKELY FACTS OF THE ANIMAL AND PLANT KINGDOMS

EVEN FISH FART!

You may not have thought about it, but fish, just like other animals, can also emit flatulence. This is possible because they too have an intestine where gas can develop, which is then often expelled in the form of a gelatinous membrane. This is precisely why, if you have an aquarium, you will not often see bubbles rising to the surface when your fish fart. However, in nature, there are fish that emit farts in the form of bubbles and even use farts to communicate with each other: these are herring. These fish are capable of sending clear signals in this way. When a herring produces a bubble of intestinal gas, it emits a high-frequency sound that attracts the attention of other herring, inviting them to form a tight school.

THE ANIMAL WITH THREE HEARTS AND NINE BRAINS!

Does this sound strange to you? Yes! There is indeed a curious animal in the depths of the sea that has not one, not two, but three hearts and nine brains.

Who are we talking about? The octopus!

The octopus has its main brain in the head and all the others distributed throughout its eight long tentacles. Indeed, the tentacles can move completely independently and autonomously, thanks to the fact that each of them has neurons. Additionally, this mollusk also has three hearts: the first two pump venous blood into the gills, while the third circulates it to the rest of the organs. And that's not all! There is another little curiosity about octopuses: while swimming, the largest heart of these octopuses stops beating. During sleep, octopuses are also capable of changing color based on what they dream about!

DID YOU KNOW THAT A "GIANT" LIVES IN THE WATER?

We are talking about a huge animal, the largest in the world. Which one? You might think of an elephant, a giraffe, or maybe a rhinoceros. Well, no! The largest animal on the planet lives in the water and it is a cetacean. It is the blue whale or "Balaenoptera musculus". This animal has unfortunately almost disappeared due to human action. Today, it is actually a protected species, and it is much less frequently seen than in the past. A few specimens have been spotted between Patagonia and Antarctica. Their habitat consists of the North Atlantic, Pacific, and Indian Oceans. These cold-water oceans are preferred by the minke whales as they find their favorite food there: krill (invertebrate marine creatures).

This enormous cetacean is considered the largest in the world with its 98.5 feet in length and its weight of 300,000 pounds. Blue whales' babies are also true giants. At birth, these calves weigh 5,000 pounds and already measure 26.2 feet long. Like many cetaceans, the minke whale also has a blowhole on its head through which it breathes by expelling jets of water. These sprays can reach a height of 29.5 feet! They are very fast swimmers. Indeed, they can reach speeds of up to 31 mph.

TURTLES BREATH THROUGH THEIR REAR END!

I guess this makes you want to burst out laughing. But you should know that turtles are probably the only animals that can also breathe through their rear end. These reptiles, like many other animals, have a mouth and lungs that allow them to breathe. However, some species of turtles prefer to absorb oxygen through another route. This is mainly due to the fact that these reptiles have a very thick and heavy shell, especially in terrestrial specimens, whose shells are quite bulky. Two of the species mainly known for this bizarre breathing are the Australian Fitzroy turtle and the North American marsh turtle.

MALE SEAHORSES CONTINUE THEIR PREGNANCY!

Here's another extraordinary curiosity from the animal kingdom: seahorses! So cute and pretty, you may see them (unfortunately) in large aquariums, or if you're lucky, in the oceans.

The male of this intriguing little animal helps his partner in every way during the reproduction process. In fact, a kind of pouch is created in his belly where the mate deposits the fertilized eggs. They will stay in the pouch with "dad" for two to eight weeks. The special event is that it is precisely the male SEAHORSE that will give birth to the young. In fact, dad has the ability to give birth to up to 1,000 baby seahorses, each measuring 0.28 inch long.

BEAVERS: "PRODUCERS OF VANILLA"

Beavers are animals that live in ponds. They have large teeth for gnawing wood and are skilled "engineers" and builders of dams. They use their large tails for a variety of purposes: to warn their fellow beavers of the presence of an enemy, as rudders when they swim, and as counterweights if they need to lift heavy objects such as tree trunks. During the Ice Age, beavers were very large animals and have since shrunk with evolution. Males are also great romantics and only love one partner for life. When they fall in love, beavers start building a new dam: that's where they'll create the nest where the new little family will live. What you may not know is that these cute rodents smell like vanilla. In fact, beavers are capable of producing a chemical substance called "Castoreum" under their tail, which gives off a vanilla scent. This completely natural chemical compound, since it is produced by animals, is also used as a flavor. In fact, it has been approved by the FDA as a food flavoring for all intents and purposes.

MONOGAMOUS ANIMALS: TOGETHER FOREVER!

Were you aware that monogamy is not a human invention, but that, just like polygamy (its opposite), it exists perfectly in nature?

It is worth knowing that there are animals that, after choosing their partner, stay together for life. This is monogamy. Some choose to mate only with their partner, such as bats; others build a real family and share the tasks of raising offspring and food procurement, notably grey wolves. You may not know it, but there are many loyal animal species! Among them is also an often underestimated animal that you probably see every day in your local parks: the pigeon. The male of this city bird takes time to find the right mate. He courts her in a long, meticulous and detailed way. Only when they are "committed" to each other is the pair stable and ready to mate. If the female agrees and feels ready to have chicks, she starts pecking the male's beak. The latter in turn, to accept the proposal, offers his mate food directly from his mouth. A bit like mother birds do to feed their chicks. Swans are also among the very romantic and faithful animals. These birds stay together for life once they form a couple. They are also very territorial and both dedicate themselves to caring for their offspring. Some birds of prey are also monogamous, including bald eagles and owls. The two form a couple for life. They are excellent parents, ready to sacrifice even their own lives to defend their young against larger predators.

DID YOU KNOW THAT DOLPHINS GET HIGH?

Dolphins are very intelligent and unique animals. One thing you should know is that these marine mammals like to get high. To do so, they absorb the venom of the pufferfish. This fish, in order to defend itself against its enemies, produces a gaseous toxin which, if inhaled in abundance, creates a narcotic effect, like a drug. Instead of being afraid of it, dolphins love this toxin. To make the pufferfish produce it, they toss the "prey" around by pushing it with their snouts, like a ball. Once the poor pufferfish releases its toxin into the water, the dolphins become intoxicated and almost enter a trance-like state. The strange cetaceans begin to feel a sense of well-being and let themselves be carried by the water, floating almost on the surface. Dolphins can "play" with a pufferfish for up to half an hour, continuing to toss it around instead of immediately eating it like they do with other species they catch. According to scientists, this confirms the fact that dolphins really do enjoy getting high in this way.

MONKEYS AT THE SPA!

Did you know that humans are not the only ones who enjoy going to spas to relax? Japanese macaques are also true relaxation enthusiasts. They enjoy wonderful natural hot springs, which are like outdoor hot water spas, not only to warm up but also to spend a nice and relaxing day. There is a particular place in Japan that is truly a paradise for these monkeys. It is called the "valley of hell" and the macaques have been living there for centuries, even braving difficult weather conditions. It is located at an altitude of 2790 feet, not far from Nagano prefecture. It is a place full of "onsen", (this word means "hot spring" in Japanese). Here, the macaques, also known as "snow monkeys", spend their day between a hot bath and a fun and mischievous snowball game, delighting visitors who climb the mountain to photograph them.

HOW DO GIRAFFES SLEEP?

Giraffes are beautiful and tall animals with long necks that live in the savannah, mainly feeding on leaves and vegetables. But have you ever wondered how they sleep? Seeing them crouched down and snuggled up for a nap is actually very rare! In fact, giraffes sleep standing up. Sleeping on the ground in a crouched position is too dangerous if you live in a place full of predators such as lions, cheetahs, hyenas... These herbivores can only allow themselves a maximum of five minutes to doze off. After that, they have to get back to an upright position to avoid putting their flesh at risk! Giraffes are the mammals that require the least amount of sleep of all. They only need half an hour of sleep per day to replenish their energy. Interestingly, until 1950, scientists believed that these animals did not sleep at all! Precisely because researchers had never seen them doze off. They also need little water. They can go three to five days without drinking. They hydrate primarily by consuming certain plants. This is an advantage because drinking from a watering place would once again be very dangerous for a giraffe. Their long neck would require them to bend down and not be able to react in the event of a predator attack.

HISTORICAL FACTS YOU MIGHT NOT KNOW!

TOXIC FASHION IN THE VICTORIAN ERA!

It may sound like a curious twist of phrase, but fashion in the Victorian era was actually toxic. We're in England. Clothing could feature many dangers: easily flammable fabrics, poisoned hairstyles, lead-laden cosmetics, breath-taking corsets and girdles, toxic dyes. Being fashionable back then was a real risk that could cost you your ass. Women, in particular, wore huge CRINOLINE skirts. Odd reports suggest that women who wore them could more easily commit theft. These skirts also had some drawbacks: on windy days, the skirts could completely turn over their structure and expose the underwear, thus filling women with shame.

Another danger of the crinoline was that it often got caught in carriage wheels and was highly flammable. It is said that a woman of the time, Frances Appleton Longfellow, perished because her dress caught fire: the flames spread so quickly that there was no time to put them out. The long dresses that women of the time wore easily became dirty on the streets, collecting mud and manure. They spread a huge amount of germs and bacteria from one place to another, bringing diseases back into the home.

Another feared curiosity was related to the color green. During the Victorian era, the chemist Carl Wilhelm Scheele invented a green pigment by mixing white arsenic, potassium, and vitriol with copper. This highly toxic and dangerous substance was enthusiastically renamed "emerald green." It became so popular that people not only used it to dye their clothes, but also to give color to candles, toys, and even candies. Think about it! The British Medical Journal claimed that women wearing green dresses could kill dozens of people at a gala. Yet none of them, despite the warnings of doctors and science, stopped wearing arsenic green. This color was appreciated and considered extremely beautiful and attractive.

THE HISTORY OF MARGHERITA PIZZA

Everyone loves pizza! When we talk about it, we immediately think of its unique taste, colors, and irresistible flavor. It is the most representative Italian dish in the country, and for many years, it has also conquered the rest of the world. Pizza has a long history dating back to ancient Egypt and Greece. But pizza, as we know it today, was born in Naples in 1738, the year when tomato was first used in its preparation. In 1889, King Umberto I and Queen Margherita visited Naples, curious to taste the typical dish of the city. It seems that the queen really enjoyed the pizza topped with mozzarella, basil, and tomatoes. Have you also noticed that the colors of these three ingredients are the same as those of the Italian flag? Since then, the pizza with this combination of toppings has been called "pizza Margherita," which is still everyone's favorite and the most popular pizza in the world.

ARE YOU FEELING A LITTLE HUNGRY?

WHO REALLY STOLE THE MONA LISA?

Leonardo da Vinci's Mona Lisa, with her delicate face and enigmatic smile, is perhaps the most famous painting of all time and one of the most representative of Italy. Leonardo painted it in Florence and then took it to France in 1516 when King Francis I offered him a job. The painting was later purchased by the king and officially became the property of France. On August 21, 1911, it was stolen from the Louvre Museum in Paris, France. And it wasn't the famous thief Arsène Lupin who stole it, but an Italian painter who worked in the museum. He deemed that the Mona Lisa belonged to Italy, so he decided to hide it under his coat and carry it away from the Louvre. He then took it to his home in the small town of Luino and hung it in his kitchen for a few years. Meanwhile, people in France and the rest of the world continued to search desperately for it. Facing financial difficulties, the thief painter decided to get rid of the painting and went to Florence in an attempt to sell it to two important antique dealers in the city. The Mona Lisa was immediately recognized, while the painter was arrested by the police. This theft contributed to making the painting even more famous throughout the world.

WHO FIRST WROTE THEIR NAME?

In school, we all learned that in Mesopotamia, the Sumerians invented writing about 5000 years ago. But who was the first person in history to write their name? The Sumerians used to write by engraving marks on clay tablets, and on one of them, a name was found: Kushim! Yuval Noah Harari, a famous Israeli historian, suggests that this man was a scribe tasked with recording quantities of barley. At the time, writing was mainly used for calculations or for cataloguing commercial information. Kushim thus became the first written name in history. The remarkable thing is that he was not a king or an emperor, but a simple wage earner. The same name was found on 12 other tablets.

UTA OF NAUMBURG: THE MOST BEAUTIFUL IN THE KINGDOM!

Do you know the evil queen from the Snow White cartoon? Well, we will now tell you who inspired the resemblance of this famous character. In the 1930s, the group of cartoonists working for Walt Disney was preparing to create what would later become the first feature-length animated film in the history of cinema. The choice of the face to give to Queen Grimhilde then met with enormous difficulties. After noting numerous sketches, the designer and director Wolfgang Reitherman spoke to Walt Disney and advised him to go to Germany, specifically to Naumburg, where there is a cathedral decorated with statues and sculptures. One of them was that of the beautiful Uta, a German noblewoman who lived around the year 1000. Needless to say, the idea was immediately welcomed with enthusiasm by everyone. Uta's face and clothing were immediately used as a model to portray the evil queen, who would now be called Grimhilde. Thanks to the Snow White cartoon, Uta's statue became world-famous.

THE FIRST NEWSPAPER IN HISTORY!

Newspapers are now part of our daily life: there are different types, and they keep us updated on everything that happens in the world. But when was the first newspaper in history published? Without a doubt, we must link the spread of the newspaper to the birth of a specific invention: movable type printing. This was developed in 1450, precisely in Germany, by Johannes Gutenberg. Thanks to this revolutionary invention, books, bulletins, newspapers, and all kinds of printed sheets began to circulate throughout Europe, every time people wanted to inform others of important news.

The first modern newspaper dates back to 1650 and was born in Leipzig, Germany, under the name "Leipziger Zeitung". The first newspaper in the United States was called "Publick Occurrences Both Forreign and Domestick" and was published in Boston, Massachusetts on September 25, 1690. However, it was shut down after its first issue because it did not have the necessary license from the colonial authorities. The first continuously published newspaper in the United States was "The Boston News-Letter", which was first printed on April 24, 1704. However, we can say that a kind of newspaper already existed several centuries earlier, in the time of the Romans. Indeed, in 59 BC, the "Decisions of the Day", that is, news informing people about the most significant events of the day, were posted on the Roman forum. They could discuss wars, political events, and sometimes even gossip!

WHY DID THE ANCIENT EGYPTIANS LOVE CATS SO MUCH?

In ancient Egypt, cats were considered sacred animals and were therefore revered and represented everywhere. From paintings to statues, everything shows us the prominent place they held in Egyptian civilization, both in religious and cultural terms. Even Mafdet (goddess of justice) or Bastet (protector of the home and symbol of fertility) were depicted in the form of a cat.

How did the Egyptians' obsession with this feline come about? One of the main reasons was the cat's ability to catch and hunt mice, snakes and parasites that could cause serious damage to crops. The friendship between the cat and man dates back about 10,000 years when the first human settlements were established along the banks of the Nile with the birth of agriculture. The cat, still as mysterious and fascinating but also very close to humans, quickly became a sacred animal, a symbol of protection and prosperity. Additionally, it was customary to embalm cats, mummify them, and place them near the tombs of kings and pharaohs to protect and watch over them in the afterlife.

THE OLDEST CARTOON IN THE HISTORY OF CINEMA!

Although Walt Disney's "Snow White" is the first feature-length animated film in history, it is not the very first cartoon ever made. The first animated film, entitled "Fantasmagorie," was directed by Emile Cohl and was shown in France on August 17, 1908. In the centuries before the invention of cinema, many experiments had been made in the world of animation. Take for instance the shadow puppet, the zoetrope, the optical theater, the kinetoscope or the magic lantern, all ingenious devices that were in a way necessary to the advent of cinema, and then of animated films. Fantasmagorie lasts two minutes in total and has no real plot: it features a clown and a stylized gentleman and many objects metamorphose under the viewer's gaze, such as a bottle that turns into a flower.

WHAT YOU DIDN'T KNOW ABOUT PRIMITIVE "HABITS"

The daily work of archaeologists and researchers, their discoveries, and numerous studies, allow us to know more and more precisely about the life and habits of our prehistoric ancestors.

Did you know that we have a lot in common with primitive humans? For example, they also had pets similar to today's dogs and cats. These animals were not only used for hunting, but were true family members, and when they died, they were buried with their owners. What else did they have in common with us? Studies have reported that they apparently also drank beer during ceremonies, cooked elaborate and delicious dishes to impress their guests, tried to follow a balanced diet based on meat and vegetables, and used knives and utensils specially designed for cooking and harvesting fruits and plants.

"COME ON, IT'S TIME TO WAKE UP!"

How did people in the early 1900s manage to get up in the morning when there were few alarm clocks on the market and most of them were very expensive? In England and Ireland, in the most industrialized cities, there was an "awakener." This unusual and widespread profession involved going around houses to wake up all the people who needed to go to work immediately. "Awakeners" were therefore armed with very long sticks that allowed them to knock on various doors until the inhabitants of the house left for work. For the same purpose, the "awakener" Mary Smith walked the streets of London with a rubber tube that she used as a blowpipe. The woman introduced dried peas and shoot them at the windows of the workers' homes. The profession of "awakener" was mainly exercised by older people or by some policemen who did it to make ends meet.

GUINNESS CURIOSITIES: THE MOST INCREDIBLE RECORDS!

Do you know the Guinness World Records book? Did you know that there are men and women in the world who are paid to find and select the craziest and most original records in the world? All these records and information are then collected. The most unique ones will have the chance to be featured in the Guinness World Records book, the grand book of records.

The first Guinness World Records Book began as a simple bet between a group of friends. Today, however, it has become a famous phenomenon all over the world. It is enough to think that the Guinness World Records Book, according to research, is the best-selling book in the world after the Bible and the Quran. In fact, there are so many curious and improbable records established every year. Let's take a look at some of the most original ones.

THE STAR WARS LEGO INSTALLATION, A RECORD!

The largest Star Wars-themed Lego installation took place in Chicago in 2019. It involved creating a giant Stormtrooper helmet out of more than 35,000 figurines.

If you haven't had the opportunity to watch Star Wars yet, Stormtroopers are the fighters of the Galactic Empire who took over the ground during the famous galactic civil war. This particular Lego work was completed in an impressive time of 38 hours, with the participation of 13 people, during the 2019 Star Wars Celebration.

THE SURFER WHO RODE THE HIGHEST WAVE IN THE WORLD!

It was November 2017 when a 39-year-old Brazilian named Rodrigo Koxa set this phenomenal record. Rodrigo managed to enter the Guinness World Records for surfing a very high wave: picture this, 82 feet! It was an exceptional feat. The young Brazilian had just broken the previous record dating back to 2011. Indeed, a 75.5-foot high wave had been crossed that year.

THE RICHEST HEIR KITTEN IN THE WORLD!

The cat's name was Blackie and it was a friendly kitten. It became the richest feline in the world after it had inherited a whopping $12.4 million after the death of its affectionate owner in 1988. Blackie was a very lucky cat. The last of a litter of 15 kittens, Blackie was adopted by its owner. This gentleman decided not to pass on his belongings and wealth to his family. Instead, he decided to bequeath all of his assets to the cat and, of course, to the people and associations that would continue to care for his beloved Blackie after his death.

RECORD-BREAKING CANDIES!

Let's focus on these desserts that break records.

Did you know that a record-breaking "panettone" was baked in Milan, the largest in the world, so big that it entered the Guinness World Records? This cake measured 4.92 feet high. Its diameter was 45.3 inches. It took about 100 hours to prepare this huge panettone, which was then officially baked in December 2018.

Sticking with sweets, let's head to Naples, and discover another record-breaking sweet treat... the world's largest zeppola di San Giuseppe! The cake was prepared for the

Father's Day celebrations on March 19, 2019. The author of this masterpiece was chef Stefano Avellano. Stefano managed to make his name in the most important book of world records, mainly thanks to a superb composition: a 55 lbs cover made of cream and sour cherries. The largest zeppola di San Giuseppe in the world weighed 185.2 lbs and had a diameter of more than 3.3 feet. A true delicacy!

Finally, another tantalizing all-Italian record, this time in Latina, Lazio, concerns profiteroles. In September 2019, this city managed to beat the Swiss record, set in March 2019, for the world's largest profiterole. The cake, composed in the Swiss town of Airola, weighed "only 507 lbs". This record was then passed on to Italy thanks to a majestic profiterole weighing 948 lbs. The profiterole is a spoon dessert that is mouth-watering. It is a cream-filled cabbage, which is then covered with a chocolate glaze. To be featured in the book of world records in Latina, a profiterole made with no less than 9,000 cream puffs, filled with 441 lbs of whipped cream, and covered with 441 lbs of chocolate was prepared.

THE LARGEST HOUSE BUILT FROM PLAYING CARDS!

This record was set by Bryan Berg in 1992. Bryan built a 75-story house using his playing cards. To build the world's tallest card castle, he used 91,800 cards in his performance. The height of the structure was 25.3 feet. Mr. Berg, once again in 2007, managed to break his own crazy record. He successfully built a very large house of playing cards that was 25.8 feet high. In 2012, he revealed in a video some of the tricks that helped him beat his record.

THE BIGGEST CHOCOLATE SMOOTHIE EXPELLED THROUGH THE NOSTRILS!

This is indeed a bizarre record established by Gary Bashaw Jr in August 1999. The star of this Guinness record is a chocolate smoothie or, as Americans call it, a "milkshake." Gary put a large amount of smoothie in his mouth and then let it out through his nostrils. The judges calculated that 1.83 oz of chocolate smoothie escaped from Mr. Bashaw's nose. They therefore awarded him a new Guinness World Record for the most amount of smoothie expelled through the nostrils!

THE LONGEST HUMAN NAILS EVER!

This record is held by a man named Mr. Melvin Boothe, whose nails in 2009 had reached a length of 32.32 feet, taking on a bizarre and phenomenal disc shape. Unfortunately, Mr. Boothe didn't have the time to improve his record as he unfortunately passed away a few months later.

GUINNESS COLLECTIONS

The place is Georgia, precisely in Alpharetta. The winner of this strange and unusual record is Mr. Val Kolpakov, who stocks the largest collection of toothpaste tubes from all over the world in his house, a total of 2037 tubes. A true Guinness World Record achieved by Kolpakov in 2012.

The "magic" record holder awarded in 2014, however, is the Mexican Menahem Asher Silva Vargas. This fellow set the record for the largest Harry Potter-dedicated collection. Would you believe that his magnificent collection has 3,092 pieces, which paved the way for his immediate entry into the world record book.

That being said, it is a woman who holds the record for the largest collection of garden gnomes. Ann Atkins entered the Guinness Book of World Records in 2000, after managing to collect 2,010 gnomes. Atkins even managed to improve on this record by expanding her collection: in 2011, she housed no less than 2,042 garden gnome statues at her home, creating a true reserve called the "Gnome Reserve". This fantastic collection is located in England, specifically in Devon, a county in the United Kingdom located on the Cornwall peninsula.

One of the noteworthy collections includes the largest collection of fast food themed "surprises" and "toys". This record was entered in the Guinness Book of World Records in 2014 when Percival Lugue requested judges to evaluate his massive collection of fast-food toys and surprises. In his home in the Philippines, in the municipality of Apalit, Percival had preserved a total of 10,000 pieces in perfect condition. He thus established the world record for the largest collection of fast-food toys.

THE ZUMBA CLASS WITH THE MOST PARTICIPANTS IN THE WORLD!

We are in the Philippines, in Mandaluyong. Here, in 2015, a huge group of 12,975 people gathered to practice zumba, the fitness practice that combines aerobic movements with music of various genres (such as hip hop, salsa, merengue, mambo...). The crowded Zumba class in Mandaluyong was thus designated by judges as "the largest ever seen in the world"...

THE LONGEST PIZZA IN THE WORLD!

Until 2017, the holders of the record for the longest pizza in the world were the Neapolitan pizza makers, but then... they were beaten! On June 10 of that year, in Los Angeles, California, local pizza makers created a pizza nearly 1.24 miles long and weighing 17,196 lbs. To prepare it, they used no less than 3,527.4 lbs of cheese and 5,604 lbs of tomato sauce.

FROM HOLLYWOOD TO HOGWARTS AND THROUGH SPACE

BUT WHO IS THIS OSCAR?

You probably already know that the Oscar is one of the most important film awards in the world. During a ceremony, which takes place every year in Hollywood, the best film, the best leading and supporting actors, the best director, the best costumes, and many other achievements are awarded a golden statuette. Everyone in Hollywood jostles to be the first to hold the famous Oscar in their hands! But how did the statuette get this name? It was born when Margaret Harrick, secretary of the Academy, saw the statuette for the first time and thought it looked a lot like... her uncle Oscar!

THE YOUNGEST WINNERS IN THE WORLD!

Throughout the history of the Academy Awards, many very young actors have received a statuette as best leading roles (but more often supporting roles) in films where they played a character. Perhaps you didn't know that some of them were very young, still kids! The youngest actress to have won an Oscar is Tatum O'Neil, who was awarded in 1974 for her performance in the film Paper Moon when she was only 10 years old. In second place is Anna Paquin, who won it in 1994 at the age of 11 for Best Supporting Actress in the film "The Piano Lessons". However, a particular record for youth in the world of cinema is held by little Mary Gibbs. The girl was a dubbing actress known for voicing some Disney characters when she was only 4 years old. Her first dubbing, however, as the "voice" of little Simba in "The Lion King - Simba's Kingdom", dates back to 1998... when she was only a year and a half old!

HARRY POTTER, THE BIG TEETH, AND THE PHILOSOPHER'S STONE!

"Harry Potter and the Sorcerer's Stone," the first movie in the hugely successful series about the small and very famous wizard, conceals some very interesting curiosities. First of all, the first scene to be filmed...was actually the last scene of the movie! That is, the one where the Hogwarts Express is leaving the magic school. In addition, the main actors were initially forced by the director to wear really uncomfortable props: Daniel Radcliffe, in the role of Harry Potter, had to wear green contact lenses because that is the color of the protagonist's eyes in the books. However, due to a severe allergic reaction, the idea had to be abandoned! On her part, Emma Watson, in the role of Hermione, played a character described in the books as having particularly large teeth. So, in the very first scenes shot, the film's director forced her to wear a very uncomfortable denture! Fortunately, she re-

60

alized that it would be impossible for her to recite her magic spells like that...and the prosthesis was removed.

WHAT YOU DIDN'T KNOW ABOUT THE LION KING

This hit Disney cartoon, released in 1994, was not inspired, like so many previous feature films, by a classic fairy tale... but rather by Shakespeare's Hamlet! The story, however, was created by incorporating many elements of the Swahili culture and language, the most spoken on the African continent (in fact, the film is set in Africa). Did you know that the name Simba means lion in Swahili? And here are the meanings of the names of the other characters: Nala means "gift", Pumba means "fool" and Rafiki means "friend". Additionally, the song "Asante sana" that the baboon Rafiki sings in a famous scene is actually a nursery rhyme from African popular culture. To top it all off, the savannah and its inhabitants were so skillfully reproduced by the designers, who before getting to work, went to prepare and relax... by treating themselves to a good African safari!

QUIET IN THE HALL!

Here are some fun facts about movie theaters from around the world that you may not know: the largest screen in the world is located at the Darling Harbour IMAX Theatre in Sydney, measuring 118 feet wide and 98.4 feet tall! What's more, the theatre can accommodate an impressive 540 people!

The typical snack to munch on at the cinema in China is dried squid, sold in packages like chips! Lastly, the oldest cinema still in operation in the world is located in France, in

61

Aniche: it's called "Idéal Cinéma-Jacques Tati" and has been open since 1905!

DINOSAURS ON THE BIG SCREEN... WITH SOME MISTAKES!

Did you know that some of the dinosaurs depicted in the first film of Steven Spielberg's Jurassic Park saga, released in 1993... never actually existed? Or rather, even if they did exist, they were very different from what you saw on screen? In particular, the velociraptor actually looked like a big chicken with a long feather-covered tail, but in the movie, it appears as a huge, fierce, muscular lizard. Then there's the dilophosaur, which in the real world, didn't spit venom at all like in the movie... and didn't have the big rainbow-colored crest it was depicted with on screen, but just a small bump on the top of its head!

UGLY ALIENS ON THE BIG SCREEN!

You've probably watched some movies in which extraterrestrials land on Earth, conquer it, become friends... or enemies of humans! There are many of them, but the most endearing movie alien is definitely the little E.T., created by Steven Spielberg and star of the 1982 film of the same name.

Did you know that the idea for the story came to the director from one of his own childhood memories? In fact, he had remembered the time when he was very young and had invented an imaginary alien friend to better cope with his parents' divorce.

Carlo Rambaldi, an Italian expert in special effects, created the appearance of E.T. and made it, according to the director's wishes, as ugly as possible. He succeeded in doing so by combining the features of famous people such as Albert Einstein with those of... a pug!

THE SCARIEST HORROR FILM IN HISTORY

In 2020, an experiment called the "**Science of Scare**" was conducted to determine the scariest horror film in history. The "**guinea pigs**" were 250 viewers who watched 30 horror films in a special room where, under the supervision of a doctor, their heartbeats were monitored during viewing. The film that caused the highest increase in their heartbeats was crowned the scariest movie ever! This was "Host," a British film released in 2020 that tells the story of a group of friends who must escape a supernatural creature generated during a video conference session. The film unfolds entirely on a Zoom video call, and despite being released only on streaming platforms, it even outperformed classics like "**The Exorcist**"!

THE MOST UNLIKELY PHOBIAS

KOUMPOUNOPHOBIA: FEAR OF BUTTONS!

In the world, there are fears that are more or less strange, which are triggered as soon as one is confronted with specific objects or situations. The origin of these fears is related to personal and traumatic events that often date back to childhood. So here are some of the most absurd fears!

Let's start with koumpounophobia, or the fear of buttons. Who would have thought that such an innocent and common object as a button could be so frightening? Some may even smile, yet this apparently unmotivated phobia can make things quite complicated. People who suffer from koumpounophobia cannot touch buttons, cannot have them on their clothing, and have trouble looking at them, even on other people! The fear of buttons is very common in young children and can be attributed to parents' fear of seeing their children swallow one or choke on it. Often, this phobia persists even into adulthood, it is linked to an excessive need for control and can cause feelings of disgust and breathlessness.

CHROMATOPHOBIA: FEAR OF COLORS!

A world without colors would be beyond imagination. However, those who suffer from chromatophobia would want to see everything in black and white, as colors are a cause of pain and suffering for them. Like all other phobias, this one stems from the association of a color with a traumatic event. This fear usually develops in relation to strong and vibrant colors. One can be afraid of all colors or of a particular color. For example, a person who is afraid of yellow (xanthophobia, from the Greek xanthos which means yellow) cannot look at any object of that color. It also seems that in many cultures and traditions, yellow is a color associated with bad luck and misfortune. People with chromatophobia generally exhibit symptoms such as strong anxiety, tachycardia, and irrational panic.

KENOPHOBIA: FEAR OF EMPTY SPACES!

Have you ever found yourself in the middle of a large empty space and immediately felt uncomfortable and particularly anxious? It could be a typical case of keno-phobia, one of the most common phobias in the world. Those who fear empty spaces feel a strong sense of anxiety and discomfort, and it doesn't matter if you're in the middle of a vast meadow or an empty room because the feeling of anxiety and fear can be the same. This phobia can manifest as a fear of flying on a plane or even leaning over a balcony. In this case as well, the causes are to be found in the traumas suffered during childhood. The symptoms of those who suffer from this fear are different and can be more or less severe depending on the person: panic, accelerated heart rate, feeling of suffocation, dizziness, nausea and headaches. In some cases, the fear of emptiness can also be understood in a metaphorical sense: the emptiness of the soul generates profound loneliness and stems from the fear of not being able to cope with a particular situation.

OMPHALOPHOBIA: FEAR OF THE NAVEL!

What are your feelings when you find yourself looking at your own navel or that of others? Are you completely indifferent or do you feel a strong sense of disgust and annoyance? Well, if you are afraid to touch or look at it, you may be suffering from omphalophobia. There are those who are afraid of direct contact with this part of the body, those who become nervous just by looking at it, those who have pain in the navel, and those who feel anxiety and panic when washing or bathing. This disorder can create serious problems, especially in the emotional and sentimental sphere. For example, try to imagine a young mother suffering from this phobia who has difficulty dressing her newborn's navel. Symptoms vary depending on the severity of the disorder, but generally, the person who suffers from it feels a strong sense of disgust and discomfort while bathing, looking at a belly button piercing, or going to places where people are undressed, such as the beach or the pool. The causes can vary with each individual case and are mainly related to painful events during birth or are associated with the fear of separation from their mother or family.

POGONOPHOBIA: FEAR OF BEARDS!

The fear of beards and mustaches is certainly one of the most absurd psychological disorders that humans suffer from, but it is also one of the most widespread in the world. The senseless phobia of bearded faces can be triggered by many factors: from the alleged lack of hygiene to the fear of bad characters in children's cartoons and fairy tales (think of Bluebeard or Pinocchio's fire-eater, for example).

Furthermore, many psychologists have observed that this phobia has significantly spread in recent years, establishing a link between pogonophobia and the fear of Islamic terrorists, one of whose distinguishing feature is a full beard. However, it seems that not everyone is fond of beards. Disdained by many famous historical figures such as Walt Disney, prohibited in some workplaces, and criticized for cultural and aesthetic reasons, the beard has long been associated with unkempt, unclean, evil and dangerous individuals.

NUMEROPHOBIA: FEAR OF NUMBERS!

Did you know that there are people in the world who are afraid of numbers and mathematics? It may sound like a joke, but it is actually a widespread pathology. The irrational fear of numbers causes a strong sense of anxiety and can seriously affect the life of the person who suffers from it. It is practically impossible to avoid numbers, as they are present everywhere in our daily lives, which forces those who suffer from this disorder to close in on themselves and isolate themselves from the world. This phobia can arise for various reasons, such as childhood traumas or real negative experiences with mathematics and arithmetic. The feeling of insecurity and the fear of making mistakes in calculations can generate states of anxiety and strong discomfort in numerophobes. Some people are afraid of a specific number like 17, 13, or 666, numbers that they associate with bad luck and religious beliefs!

AMBULOPHOBIA: FEAR OF WALKING!

Although it is an uncommon phobia, ambulophobia is a very particular and limiting condition. The person affected is terrified at the mere thought of walking, or rather, afraid of falling, and therefore avoids moving their legs to get around. It is a widely prevalent phobia, especially among older people, although anyone can suffer from it. After walking without any problem throughout their life, it may happen that a person, following an operation, a fall, or a terrible accident, feels so uncomfortable that they are unable to move around unless they have the help of a cane or other support. There are people who are afraid of walking on any surface, and those who feel so vulnerable and unsure of themselves that they never leave their homes.

TRICHOPHOBIA: FEAR OF HOLES!

If you have ever been terrified by the sight of objects with holes and cavities, you are trypophobic. People with this disorder experience an uncontrollable feeling of aversion and fear when they see, for example, a beehive, a polka dot dress, or a bath sponge. In short, anything with holes, openings, and protrusions can be frightening and provoke unpredictable reactions. The more holes there are, the stronger the fear. This is a very common condition, but little is known about it, and it is the subject of international studies. Experts tend to make a distinction between phobia and fear: while a phobia is an excessive terror of something that is actually harmless and causes no physical harm, fear is a normal and instinctive reaction that occurs in the face of danger or something threatening. At this point, why does the trypophobic person have a fear of holes? It may be an instinctive defense mechanism against things that resemble snake scales, infectious diseases, or hiding places of dangerous animals.

KEROPHOBIA: FEAR OF HAPPINESS!

If we talk about kerophobia, many people may think of the title of a famous musical refrain that was released a few years ago. But what is the fear of happiness and why should anyone be afraid of happiness? There are people in the world who are afraid of being happy and experiencing intense emotions. Feeling joy and enthusiasm can be perceived as a moment of weakness and vulnerability.

Kerophobes tend to defend themselves against these emotions. Those who suffer from it view happiness as a threat, which can cause anxiety and restlessness. Their logical thought pattern is as follows: if you're happy, be careful because you'll likely suffer soon. Kerophobes fear that their happiness will come to an end sooner or later, so they avoid experiencing it altogether. They avoid participating in enjoyable events, feel anxious in the presence of happy people or those who appear to be happy, and have a negative and pessimistic attitude toward life and emotions. Childhood traumas, humiliations, and painful events are among the main causes of this condition. That's why kerophobia becomes a defense mechanism against something that could hurt them sooner or later.

NOMOPHOBIA: FEAR OF BEING DISCONNECTED!

The truth is that we don't know how to be without our phone. The smartphone is now a part of our daily lives, and going without it would seem strange, if not unthinkable. But there are people in the world who simply can't do without it. Such people suffer from nomophobia, which in addition to being considered one of the strangest and most absurd phobias ever, is also considered by many to be the fear of the 21st century.

NOMOPHOBIA

(from the English "no mobile phone phobia") is nothing but the fear of being without an internet connection. Some may smile, but we are dealing with a "childish" fear of our time: the real fear is not so much losing one's smartphone or breaking it, but not being able to connect to the rest of the world. If the phone is dead or unable to connect to the network, it can cause the nomophobic person to experience states of anxiety and high agitation. Without the internet, the person affected risks feeling alone and cut off from the world. We are dealing with a real disconnection syndrome!

Curiosities about
the human body

BETWEEN TRINKETS AND SUPERPOWERS!

WHAT HAPPENS IF YOU EAT BOOGERS?

Your nose is capable of much more than you think. How many smells do you think you can recognize? A hundred, a thousand? Hang on: the human nose is capable of distinguishing about a trillion different odors. In addition, we are able to remember them much more accurately than images (we remember 65% of them after one year, compared to 50% for images). However, the sense of smell can also be faulty: some people suffer from parosmia, a distorted sense of smell that leads them to "confuse" perceived odors with others. Others suffer from "phantosmia": the perception of "phantom" smells that are not actually present in the environment.

And the initial question, do you want us to answer it? First, we must ask ourselves what is in boogers: what do they contain? They consist of dehydrated mucus, which may also contain enzymes, antibodies, and fats. But that's not all!

Mucus is a defense tool of the body, whose function is precisely to "trap" bacteria and other microorganisms such as

71

viruses and fungi. For this reason, if you eat boogers... they are good for you! They stimulate your immune system, making them healthy for your body.

IS IT TRUE THAT EATING CARROTS MAKES YOU TAN MORE?

We'll tell you right away: it's false! There are no foods that can truly stimulate tanning, but you should keep in mind that tanning is is one way our skin protects itself from the sun's harmful rays. In fact, when we expose ourselves to the sun, the skin cells produce melanin, a dark <u>PIGMENT</u> that forms a protective layer against the sun's rays. Beta-carotene, found in carrots as well as in many other vegetables such as tomatoes and spinach, also contributes to protecting the skin, which reinforces this action.

WHY SHOULD YOU LET YOUR BEARD GROW?

Maybe the question isn't relevant to you right now, but in a few years... and only if you're a man, of course! However, don't forget that letting your beard grow can be beneficial to your health. Don't believe it? To start with, the beard helps protect the skin on your face from harmful solar radiation. It slows down aging too, since it's also the sun's rays that cause wrinkles to appear! In addition, the beard "filters" microorganisms such as bacteria, which have a harder time reaching the covered area. It effectively protects us from both the cold and excessive heat!

RULES FOR A PERFECT NIGHT'S SLEEP!

It is very important to have a sound night's sleep: you may already know that sleep is essential to maintaining the balance of all the processes in our body and allowing it to recover after exertion.

To sleep well at night, we can help ourselves... with a nap during the day! 15 to 20 minutes of sleep in the afternoon can improve our stress management and allow us to arrive in the evening feeling more "refreshed" and therefore better prepared to sleep at night. Here are some other tips for better sleep: walk for at least 15 minutes after dinner and... sleep in your own bed! Indeed, if you sleep away from home, your brain remains more alert to perceive potential dangers... and you don't rest well!

WOLVERINE'S DNA!

Do you know Wolverine, the character from the X-men comic series, equipped with an adamantium skeleton that makes him invulnerable? Well, you should know that there are real superheroes in the world who are very similar to him. A genetic mutation in a particular gene called LRP5 makes the bones of some people practically indestructible, with a dense, heavy, and fracture-resistant skeleton. Scientists at the Yale School of Medicine discovered this phenomenon by studying a family that had never experienced bone problems in generations!

WHAT IS SO SPECIAL ABOUT OUR BRAIN?

A lot, actually! For example, it is so active that it alone consumes 20% of all the oxygen that flows into our body, and it never stops... not even at night! In fact, when we sleep, brain activity is more intense than during the day (and our dreams or nightmares depend on it!). The possibilities of our brain are incredibly vast and still largely untapped: not long ago, it was believed that our brain was capable of storing five times the information contained in an encyclopedia if we wanted it to. Nowadays, scientists estimate that a human brain could store 1 petabyte of data, which is equivalent to 1 million billion bytes, or 1,000 times the capacity of a modern PC hard drive, or if you prefer, the equivalent of the content of 5 billion books! And what if by developing the still "dormant" areas of the brain, humans were capable of doing something else, like... moving objects with just their thoughts?

A CAR-PROOF STOMACH!

Gastric juice is a clear liquid present in our stomach that helps us digest food. It contains several elements, such as water, bicarbonate, potassium, sodium, but the real bomb, the number one enemy of heavy and indigestible foods, is... hydrochloric acid! It's a highly corrosive liquid (in fact, if there's too much of it in your stomach, you can suffer from gastritis and heartburn), but incredibly powerful: according to the writer Isaac Asimov, who was also a biochemist, hydrochloric acid could dissolve a tissue paper, but also the bodywork of a car! However, we do not recommend eating a car.

YOUR HAIR IS STRONGER THAN HULK!

Here's something you didn't know about your hair: if you let them grow your entire life without ever cutting them, they could reach a length of about 621.4 miles (to better understand, the distance between New York and Ottawa heading north!). Moreover, they are incredibly resistant: to break a hair, you have to pull it very hard, stretching it one and a half times its length. This makes it more resistant than a copper wire of the same diameter! By the way, the visible part of the hair... is the dead part! The only living part is the one still inside the skull, waiting to sprout.

DON'T PRICK YOUR EARS!

Treat your ears well! Besides being a very delicate organ, it hides many secrets: first of all, the fact that it will continue to grow throughout your life... even when you are an adult! Don't worry, you won't end up like Dumbo: they grow about 0.008 inch per year, which is approximately 0.04 inch in 50 years. They also contain the smallest bones in the body: the anvil, the hammer, and the stirrup. Finally, did you know that in addition to loud sounds, absolute silence is also very, very uncomfortable for the ear? This was proven in an experiment conducted at the Orfield Labs in Minneapolis, USA. That's where the zero-noise chambers were created: anyone who entered them started to hear all the sounds of their body, including their heartbeat... and couldn't wait to get out!

BEWARE OF PHANTOM ODOR!

Your nose is capable of much more than you think. How many scents do you think you can recognize? A hundred, a thousand? Hang on: the human nose can distinguish about a trillion different odors. Moreover, we are able to remember them much more accurately than images (we remember them 65% after a year, compared to 50% for images). However, the sense of smell can also be defective: some people suffer from parosmia, a distorted sense of smell that leads them to "confuse" perceived odors with others. Then there's "phantosmia": the perception of "phantom" odors, which are not actually present in the environment!

CONCLUSION

Dear boys and girls, we have come to the end of this amazing tour of curiosities and incredible facts that you probably didn't know. I hope that this compilation has enabled you to spend some pleasant time, but above all to satisfy your thirst for knowledge and originality.

As promised, you will find a small glossary containing some of the more difficult terms used within these pages. And of course, all that's left to do is to put yourself to the test with the "Final Quiz"! Challenge yourself and your relatives to finish this enjoyable read in an equally entertaining way.

Cheers to all!

GLOSSARY

Crinoline: fabric for women's clothing made from horsehair

Phobia: a pathological fear, often without any apparent reason;

Hotspot: a connection point that allows access to the internet via Wi-Fi;

Seashore: synonym of hippocampus;

Octopod: a class of mollusks with eight legs;

Pigment: a substance that dissolves in a liquid and turns colored;

Fate: a fact of chance, or of a supposed predestination;

Theobromine: a substance found in cocoa in the form of powder, colorless and bitter;

Toxin: a substance of animal or vegetable origin that can be harmful;

Boulangerie viennoise: traditional bakery in Vienna.

THE FINAL TRIVIA QUIZ

Now that you've read so much trivia, are you ready for a game?

Challenge your friends and family to answer the "Final Quiz" questions correctly.

For each question, you have three answer options: try to figure it out but remember, only one is right!

In case you have any doubts, don't worry, you will find the correct answers at the end of the quiz.

Whoever comes up with the most correct answers will be the winner of the quiz!

Ready to go? All right!

Let the QUIZ begin!

1) How many hearts does an octopus have?

A. 1
B. 3
C. 2

2) What is the world's most stolen food?

A. Chewing gum
B. Pizza
C. Cheese

3) What color in the Victorian era was a "toxic" pigment?

A. Yellow
B. Green
C. Blue

4) How many hours a week does the Cuiva work?

A. 5 to 10 hours
B. 15 to 20 hours
C. 30 to 40 hours

5) Which reptile species prefers to breathe through the rear of its body?

A. Turtle
B. Snake
C. Crocodile

6) What does "Rafiki" mean in Swahili?

A. Monkey
B. Sorcerer
C. Friend

7) In which country was the world's largest profiterole award handed out in 2019?

A. S Switzerland
B. Italy
C. France

8) Which animal's characteristic features were used in designing the appearance of the alien E.T.?

A. An elephant
B. A pug
C. A baboon

9) To which category do peanuts belong?

A. Impulses
B. Nuts
C. Fruits

10) In the record-breaking 2019 Star Wars installation, what did they build with Lego?

A. A lightsaber
B. Princess Leia
C. A Stormtrooper helmet

11) To what pollinating insect do we owe thanks if we enjoy chocolate?

A. The fly
B. The mosquito
C. The hornet

12) Which spice was also used for paying rent in the Middle Ages?

A. Salt
B. Sugar
C. Black pepper

13) From which country do the "croissants" originate?

A. France
B. Italy
C. Austria

14) In Colombia, how do the Nukak people get their hair cut?

A. With tiger teeth
B. With piranha teeth
C. With shark teeth

15) Why was a hotspot set up on Everest?

A. To help climbers in case of emergency
B. To connect to social media
C. To order food from home

16) In India, what does the Solima tribe leave for the tigers?

A. A fruit
B. Fish
C. Honey

17) Which medieval noblewoman inspired the character of the evil queen in Snow White?

A. Queen Elizabeth
B. Uta of Naumburg
C. Sophia of Prussia

18) Who stole the Mona Lisa from the Louvre Museum on August 21, 1911?

A. An Italian painter
B. Arsenio Lupin
C. German soldiers

19) In Brazil, which question is usually asked when you are invited to someone's house?

A. Hello, how are you?
B. Can I offer you a cup of tea?
C. Would you like to take a shower?

20) Where is Atacama Desert, famous for being the driest in the world?

A. In Mexico
B. In Chile
C. In Algeria

SOLUTIONS

1: B	8: B	15: A
2: C	9: A	16: C
3: B	10: C	17: B
4: B	11: A	18: A
5: A	12: C	19: C
6: C	13: C	20: B
7: B	14: A	

BOOK 2

ASTONISHING INVENTIONS FOR CURIOUS KIDS

INTRODUCTION

Have you ever wondered who invented the microwave or the shopping cart? Or even who discovered the eraser and the chalkboard?

After savoring a delicious portion of French fries, have you ever felt the curiosity to discover how could such a delicacy came to be?

We're all curious. This is how human beings are naturally created; that's a given fact. A light bulb goes on in our brain and we feel the urge to know something. It really happens to everyone, big or small. It's even more common for kids, who have an immeasurable desire to know about everything. They are like little sponges, ready to absorb every bit of information. And do you know why? Because they are writing down their knowledge, day after day, and they're doing it with our help, the help of their parents.

Children are eager to learn, to understand, to know! And this is an ongoing challenge for us as parents too. We are consumed with the desire to pass on what we know to our children, the adults of tomorrow, the ones we can call "our future". That's what children are: our future. And this is why we need to preserve them and take care of them. This is all about evolution: passing knowledge from one generation to another, so that every generation is a little more evolved than the previous one. We consider this a challenge that keeps us busy every day and keeps us alive.

In this book, you will find a collection of surprising discoveries that will intrigue your children. Starting from how some

84

foods kids (and not just them!) love, such as Coca-Cola or ice cream, came about almost accidentally, to how some of the everyday tools they use at school were created, such as the pencil, the pencil sharpener, and school desks. They will also find out where their favorite games come from, such as basketball. We will also point out many curious inventions of everyday objects that are used daily by all of us that we now take for granted. Let's think about matches, toothbrushes, or the TV.

We are Linda and Charlie, happy parents of two wonderful kids, and creators of the Kairoslandd project.

We both work and live in this hectic society, which made us painfully aware that we could only have very little time to spend with our babies. We realized that they were growing and that we weren't always able to be there in the most important phases of their journey, or at any rate we literally had to jump through hoops to be able to attend a school play, a dance recital or a soccer game.

We understood we could never get back the time we were losing as a result of life, commitments, and worries. Therefore, we decided to find a way to make the best of the time we could realistically dedicate to our children. And this is also how it came to mind to create Kairoslandd.

Kairoslandd was created for parents who wanted to be there at "the right time" and fill a virtual scrapbook with incredible emotions so that they wouldn't slip away.

This is not an in-depth scientific or technical book but rather a collection of curiosities about the discoveries and inventions that have changed our existence. It's an informational text whose aim is not only to stimulate childrens' curiosity, but also provide some potential answers to questions that many of us have asked ourselves when looking at a daily-life object. We often wonder: "Who discovered or invented it?"

Ok, we won't keep you waiting any longer. Follow us throughout the first chapter, where we will talk about food and where you, as kids and parents, will discover how so many delicacies often unexpectedly discovered or invented by chance have come to be!

ARE YOU READY?

Then let's all go on a journey together, shall we?

Happy reading!

FOOD. SO MANY SURPRISING DELIGHTS!

> *The discovery of a new dish does more for the happiness of humanity than the discovery of a star.*
> *(Jean Anthelme Brillat-Savarin)*

We can make ourselves comfortable at the table now and start to taste many unexpected delicacies. But before biting into our fries and taking a sip of our Coca-Cola, let's ask ourselves: "What would our lives be like if nobody had discovered certain meals we enjoy so much?". Luckily, some people did indeed discover delicacies such as ice cream and chocolate chip cookies... but who are they?

We are now going on an imaginary (but not but not so crazy) trip back in time by poking around in history, both recent and past, to learn who discovered or invented all those foods we adore. Are you ready? Then, let the adventure begin!

FRENCH FRIES

This is one of the foods most of us love. French fries were unintentionally invented in 1853 by George Crum, a New York chef. Do you want to know how it all happened? Legend has it that a very rich and picky restaurant client complained about the potatoes he was served and decided to send the dish back to the kitchen three times with the excuse that the potatoes were cut too thick. Crum was so displeased that he started preparing a fourth dish where cut the potatoes so thin and made them so crisp that it would have been impossible to eat them with a fork (as was the custom, at the time). He also covered them with an excessive amount of salt. Surprisingly, the customer not only stopped complaining but was so enthusiastic about the novelty that he ordered a second portion. This is how French fries were born, were passed down to us and became famous for being an appetizing snack for people both young and old.

COCA-COLA

We bet you love this famous drink, which was discovered by accident as well. Indeed, better yet, it was born with another purpose. It was a May evening in 1886 when the Atlanta pharmacist John Stith Pemberton created a plant-extract- and kola-nut- (an African tree) based recipe. Using a brass boiler and his desire to invent a syrup to cure headaches, the U.S. pharmacist had unintentionally created the recipe for the world's most famous drink.

THE LOLLIPOP

Have you ever tried Tootsie Pops? They're the delicious candy that you enjoy on a tiny stick. Well, that can be defined as the last version of a lollipop, but if we want to go back to its birth, we have to go back to find our ancestors: primitive men. Yes, you heard us! Stone-Age men collected honey with a stick and ate it directly from there. This may have been the first lollipop in history. It's a tasty treat that certainly didn't disappear until the following centuries: in Russia, in 1489, animal-shaped lollipops came out. After that, we travel back in time again and get to Europe, where they became popular in the 19th century as sweet balls strung on a stick. Later, in 1916, Samuel Born, a Russian who emigrated to the United States, invented a machine to produce lollipops on a large scale. Despite this widespread use, George Smith is universally recognized as the inventor of the modern lollipop, who patented the lollipop in 1916. The most famous lollipop in the world, however, remains the Chupa Chups, produced by Spanish confectioner Enric Bernat in 1958 and popularized under the name "Gol".

CHOCOLATE CHIP COOKIES

What about taking a little break with a nice chocolate chip cookie? We are sure you love this snack too. Who doesn't? What are you saying? *Mom lets you have them as a snack after school homework?*

Well, moms sure know what their children love... moms know a lot of things.

But have you ever wondered who invented them? She was a mom! Her name was Ruth Jones Graves Wakefield. It was 1937 when Ruth and her husband ran an inn called Toll House Inn and she used to cook for guests. Legend says that Ruth realized that she ran out of dark chocolate while she was preparing cookie dough so, just like every mom does, she ingeniously replaced the chocolate with a semi-sweet bar. She cut it into pieces and put it in the dough, hoping it would melt like chocolate. The bar, though, didn't melt and cookies were baked with those little chocolate chips that made their fortune. This is how Ruth Wakefield invented chocolate chip cookies, the cookies that have become a favorite among Americans and many others around the world.

ICE CREAM

Even in this case, to discover the origins of the ice cream, another treat we are sure you love, we have to go back in time. Long agao, there is a trace of it even in ancient peoples, from those who lived in Mesopotamia, and China, to those in ancient Egypt and ancient Rome. The ancestors of ice cream as we know it consisted mainly of fruit drinks or foods sweetened with honey and mixed with ice or snow, so they did not have the creamy consistency that today's ice creams have. Moving on to the Middle Ages, it was mainly the Arabs who consumed iced foods (in fact, they also invented the sorbet). It was, however, in the 17th century that the consumption of iced foods in the courts spread greatly, and milk and eggs were also added to the basic ingredients. And this is how we get to Francesco Procopio dei Coltelli, who in 1686 left Sicily in search of fortune, which he found in Paris, opening the first ice cream shop. He fined tune the recipe for ice creams, sorbets, and granitas, which he made with machines he invented himself. He is considered the father of modern ice-cream still today.

THE POPSICLE

Who doesn't love a nice fruit popsicle during a hot summer afternoon? Yes, I know you love popsicles, but I also bet you don't know that it was an 11-year-old boy who invented this tasty and fresh delicacy. It was a kid named Frank Epperson who, quite accidentally, discovered the popsicle.

It was 1905 when little Frank had the brilliant idea of saving his pocket change by giving up purchasing ready-made sodas and making one himself at home. He decided to mix water and soda to create an effervescent drink. Because of his carelessness, however, Frank forgot the glass with the drink still in it and the stick with which he had mixed it on the windowsill. The next morning the little boy received a nice surprise, the mixture had frozen, and he had invented the popsicle.

If you enjoyed this brief journey in which we discovered how many of the foods we still find delicious were born, keep following us in the next chapter where we will discover how so many items you use daily were created. These are related to an environment you know very well: school.

SCHOOL: FROM CLAY TABLETS TO CALCULATORS

> **During my nine years in high school, I failed to teach my professors anything.**
> **(Bertolt Brecht)**

You may have become worried after reading the title of this chapter. Don't worry, we won't be boring while talking about school. Over the next few pages, we want to share with you some discoveries we got to know about school and everything related to this institution, the Achilles' heel for students like yourself.

If you have ever asked yourself who invented school (and we are pretty sure you have at least once), or even who invented all those tools you use daily during your school hours, you've come to the right place.

In the following paragraphs, you will discover not only how the school as you know it was invented, but also the inventor of the pencil sharpener and the eraser, and you'll find out who invented something that facilitates your work like the calculator or who invented the Braille alphabet, which provides a reading tool for blind children to read with others during school lessons. Are you ready to delve into the world of school from a different perspective? Off we go on another adventure together, this time discovering everything about school.

92

THE SCHOOL

As a first step, we must begin with the very people who invented the school. School is, in fact, a very ancient institution. Consider that the Greek word *scholèion* (from which the Latin for *schola* comes) originally meant "free time". Incredible, isn't it? Over time, the meaning has slightly changed because it became a place where science and philosophy were discussed, precisely during leisure time. Later on, the latter also changed to mean "a place where people read" and it eventually became "a place where things are learned".

The educational system was invented by the Sumerians, practically immediately following the invention of writing, that is, around 3,500 B.C., and the schools were called *edubba* ("house of tablets") because they wrote on wet clay tablets, which were then dried in the sun and baked. In these schools, people learned to read, write, and do math. This was the school model that was also later adopted in Mesopotamia and ancient Egypt.

It was between the 5th and 6th century B.C. that a less rigid school system was founded in ancient Greek, and was reserved only for a few fortunate ones. In ancient Rome, the first education system was passed on by the mother, then the father, and only a few chosen pupils had the opportunity to have a private teacher or go to school before they learned to read, write, and count.

In ancient Rome, girls, unlike in other civilizations, could attend school, but only until they turned fifteen because it was then time to get married. The first state-organized schools, which may be the ancestors of modern schooling, began to emerge around the 18th century.

In Italy, the record of the first organization of state schools is held by what was then the Kingdom of Sardinia. It was Maria Theresa of Austria who in 1774 established compulsory schooling for children between the ages of six and 12. In France, primary schooling became compulsory soon after the French Revolution, and in the rest of Europe, it was not until the nineteenth century that free public compulsory schools were available. The Pencil

The first pencils were made in 1564 in England, soon after graphite was discovered. We don't know who the inventor is, but in 1795 the chemist Nicolas Conté developed and patented a process used to produce pencils, based on a clay and graphite mixture, which had to be fired in a kiln before being placed in a wooden case. This method made it possible to produce various types of pencils, both hard and soft ones, something very important considering the possibilities artists and draftsmen had. The first pencil factory in the USA was built in New York by Eberhard Faber in 1861.

THE ERASER

Rubber as a substance is very old, but it was the scientist Charles Marie de La Condamine who brought this natural substance to France in 1736 from South America.

It was used by South American Indians either to make game balls that could bounce and as glue for feathers or objects. It was Edward Naime, in 1770, who was credited to be the inventor of the eraser.

In that period, people used breadcrumbs to erase pencil marks and it was Naime who stated that he accidentally picked up a piece of rubber instated of bread and thus discovered that it could erase pencil marks.

This is how rubber cubes were used to erase. There was a small problem though: the natural rubber went bad. It got rotten just like food, so it was not easy to work with it as it was.

It was finally in 1839 thanks to Charles Goodyear that a method was discovered to process rubber and make it durable and usable by a process he called vulcanization.

Goodyear patented his process in 1844. The first patent for attaching an eraser to a pencil can be credited to Hyman Lipman of Philadelphia in 1858, a patent that was canceled, however, because it was deemed unoriginal, Lipman had merely combined two things but that couldn't have been aimed at a new purpose other than what they already had.

THE PENCIL SHARPENER

Staying on topic: have you ever wondered who invented the pencil sharpener? It's such a useful object, especially the ones with a container. How brilliant!

Well, the pencil sharpener derives directly from the sharpener, which was originally used to sharpen pencils. The first patent application for a pencil sharpener dates to 1828 and was made by the French mathematician Bernard Lassimone. But it was Thierry des Estwaux in 1847 who invented the manual pencil sharpener as we know it. Finally, it was in November 1897 that John Lee Love of Massachusetts patented the "Love Sharpener", the pencil sharpener with a container like the one you still use in school today.

MARKERS AND HIGHLIGHTERS

They're in your pencil case, aren't they? They surely are since they seem to be indispensable for going to school. Have you ever asked yourself who invented them?

Well, the first felt-tip marker, which then became the one we all know today, was probably born in 1940 but was primarily for writing on labels.

In 1952 Sidney Rosenthal started to sell his "Magic Marker", as he called it, which consisted of a little glass bottle containing ink and a wick made of wool felt.

In 1958 markers had become virtually commonplace and they were used to write, label, and mark packages, as well as to make posters.

Fine-tip highlighters and markers came to be during the 70s, in the same period when permanent-ink-markers also became available.

In the 90s, the super-fine-tipped markers and erasable markers became popular, when the Avery Dennison Corporation registered the patent for the "Hi-Liter" pen, the famous highlighter.

GEL PENS

We are sure you have some of of these in your pencil case as well: gel-ink-pens. This was another tool that became very popular among students.

Gel ink was invented in 1984 by Sakura Color Products Corp. of Osaka, Japan. It's an ink with a gel-like consistency that uses water-soluble color pigments. The company also launched Gelly Roll pens in 1984. The same company, back in 1925, invented the oil crayon, combining oil and color pigment, introduced to the market under the name Cray-Pas.

THE SCHOOL BACKPACK

Let's talk about your school backpack now! How could you carry all the items we've been talking about so far to school every morning without it? Yours must be the latest model, a fashionable backpack indeed, but do you know who invented the school backpack and when? During the Middle Ages, there was a sort of ancestor of the backpack. Tn fact, kids carry what they needed for school in woven baskets held together by ropes.

For this reason alone, just think how lucky you are! Children began using them in the late 40s, and after the end of World War, the materials available also made bags more functional, lightweight, and practical.

It was 1952 when the first modern conceived backpack was invented by Dick Kelty, a hiker who wanted to create an alternative sketch just out of passion, which could have been more effective and comfortable to the military gear that was used for hiking back then. Kelty kept on working on his idea, improving it more and more and in the 70s his backpacks gained popularity among sportsmen. In 1967, then, Greg Lowe invented the internal backpack frame.

SCHOOL DESKS

Here you have another question we are sure you have asked yourself quite a few times while sitting at your desk in the classroom: who invented those desks? If you consider what we said a couple of pages earlier, going to school wasn't obligatory before the 19th century and children studied at home and they did it sitting at any table, like the one you have in your kitchen. But those who studied in a real school did it while sitting at a long wooden table or directly on benches without a desk, reading and writing while holding books directly on their legs. It wasn't until the 1880s that American John Loughlin thought of making desks specifically designed for kids, so they were smaller in size to be devoted to study hours. Loughlin was the founder of the Sidney School Furniture Company, which made the first school desks, calling them "fashion desks". They were made following the conformation of the body and were one body, table, and chair attached. They had space for the inkwell and up to three students could sit on each bench. The patent under the name "school desks" was registered by Anna Breadin in 1889 although Loughlin and the Sidney School Furniture Company continued to produce them and supply schools. In the early 20th century, school desks would begin to evolve, partly due to the introduction of many school textbooks, to meet the new requirements, the table began to have a liftable top, and a shelf was placed underneath it to store books and school supplies. Time went by and schools began to be attended by more and more children. They needed larger desks. The "Welsh desk school" was meant for two students to occupy side by side and had a double shelf. In the 30s, desks could also be adjusted vertically and allowed the chair to be rotated. However, the school desk continued to evolve until the 70s, and wood was gradually replaced with less expensive materials, such as plastic.

THE BLACKBOARD

Here we have another tool that has been in schools for a very long time: the blackboard. Have you ever caught yourself wondering who created this valuable support for teachers? Or do you know why it's called this? Well, let's answer both curiosities.

The blackboard was introduced as a teaching tool in the early 1800s by an American preacher named Samuel Read Hall. Precisely in 1823, Hall was freshly appointed and boasted a few years of teaching in his experience. From New Hampshire he was transferred to Concord, a tiny town in Vermont, to exercise his role as pastor. Once he arrived in the small town, he realized that both the school and the church were small and unsuitable for the purpose they would serve. So, he asked if he could conduct training courses for teachers in the area. Relying on a salary of $300 a year, he was able to establish the Columbian School, America's first school dedicated to teacher training, and there he began to teach classes and seminars.

It was during his lectures that he introduced a teaching method that he had personally devised during his early teaching experiences. To illustrate the lessons, he explained he used a dark-colored slab of soft rock on which he wrote with a piece of chalk. It was a method, that for its time, was decidedly avant-garde and was slowly adopted by the entire teaching world and would not leave classrooms for the next two centuries.

In addition, Hall called it a blackboard, because the stone slabs of which it is made consist of slate, also known as the "blackboard stone". Something interesting is that he would never recognize himself as an inventor but only as a churchman and educator, and this is who he decided to be for the rest of his life.

COLORED CHALK

Chalk itself is not an invention, considering that it exists in nature since immemorial time, being made of prehistoric saltwater organisms enriched with calcium that went on to form rock-like sediments.

Since numerous chalk-based materials had been used for writing over the centuries, we don't have an actual inventor of natural chalk, but we know who discovered how to color it. Conventionally, the discovery dates back to Scottish James Pillans, who was a geography teacher and the principal of the Old Royal High School of Edinburgh. Back then, the blackboard had already become commonplace in classrooms and Pillans used a recipe based on chalk, dyes, and porridge to color the natural chalk. The Calculator

Are you familiar with the calculator? That tool that makes you do math quickly but that your parents insist on telling you not to use because you need to practice doing math in your head? We agree with your parents: you need to exercise your brain and learn how to do math yourself. On the other hand, how could we deny that it was indeed a phenomenal and convenient invention (and not only for students)?

Well, you won't believe this, but the first calculator or, rather, its ancestor, was invented in 1648 by a very young boy named Blaise Pascal (he was a French mathematician, physicist, philosopher, and theologian, as well as a child prodigy. He wrote a treaty on geometry when he was only ten years old). Pascal invented a mechanical calculator that was able to do additions and subtractions and called it "the Pascaline".

AN ALPHABET FOR THE BLIND

This very useful invention comes from a very young mind as well, that of Louis Braille. The writing and reading system for blind people is still called the "Braille alphabet". Little Louis, when he was only three years old, injured his left eye, and the infection quickly spread to his right eye, making him completely blind.

In 1821, when he was only twelve years old, Braille had a flash of inspiration and created the writing and reading method for blind people that would gradually become famous all over the world.

The idea came to him during a school lesson where a military man was a guest speaker who explained a method of message transmission used by the armed forces that was based on twelve raised dots. Within a few years, Louis Braille perfected a system based on six dots, and this became the universally used writing and reading system for blind people that is still used around the world today.

We hope you enjoyed this brief journey through history to discover how so many of those tools you still use today at school came to be. After having immersed us in the school world, we will now look for those who invented (or discovered) many things related to an area of your life we're sure you'll enjoy even more: games and leisure.

GAMES AND LEISURE. DO YOU REMEMBER PLAYING WITH THE PONGO?

> **Today I'm doing nothing because I started doing it yesterday and I wasn't finished.**
> **(Peanuts, Charles M. Schulz)**

Here we are, my dear friend, ready to delve into this other world, that of games and leisure: two activities I'm sure you love doing as well. Let's be honest — everyone deserves a little bit of leisure and fun after all those hours of school and study.

Let me ask you a question: Would you rather play outdoors? Maybe you're lucky enough to have a nice garden outside your house to have fun with your friends. Or, do you prefer to play indoors? Maybe you like playing video games? Do you practice any sports, such as basketball? We are sure you are keen on everything we just mentioned, and you surely have in mind many other ways to have fun, whether indoors or outdoors, just like playing board games with friends or taking some nice bike rides. If we had to list all the possible ways to have fun, we could write an endless list. Have you ever wondered who discovered or invented most of the amusements or games that you know as well? Who invented basketball, who created video games? Who discovered the Pongo, the playdough I'm sure you played with sometimes? Who brought a phenomenal and fun invention like the bicycle into our lives?

Well, make yourself comfortable because in this chapter we'll once again take you on a journey into the past to answer these questions and many more. Are you ready? Let's not wait anymore and begin our journey back in time...

THE TRAMPOLINE

You won't believe this, but the invention of the trampoline is attributed to a young boy, George Peter Nissen, who was a great gymnast. It was 1934, Nissen was twenty years old, and he did not only invent the trampoline as we know it, but he also made it a worldwide sport, managing to include it in the Olympic games. Considering that he kept building trampolines with his own company, his daughter Dian also became a champion in this sport.

George built his first trampoline in his parents' garage with makeshift materials. Intending to improve his performance and training better, he created a steel structure and attached a net to it. The first name of his invention was "rebound facility", a name that perfectly explained its purpose. Later on, he renamed his invention "trampoline", the name that it's still called today.

BASKETBALL

This fun and healthy team game was also born by accident, or perhaps we should say 'out of some sort of necessity'. It was 1891 when James Naismith, a Canadian P.E. teacher living in the United States and working at Springfield College in Massachusetts invented this game.

Winter months in Massachusetts are tough, so he had to find a way to keep his students busy while having them practice inside the gym. The teacher, being inspired by a game he used to play as a kid, called *Duck-on-a-rock*, which consisted of shooting a rock in a parabola, thus came up with a simple game by hanging a basket (an improvised and rudimentary hoop) on the wall and invited his students to throw a ball into it. Two weeks later, Naismith wrote and presented to the whole college the rules of what would become one of the most popular sports in the world. When popularity of the game started to spread, they had to solve the problem of retrieving the ball, which they had to take out of the basket using a ladder. That's when they decided to cut off the lower part of it, so that the ball could fall back to the ground through the hole. During the 20th century, a net started to be used and still is. Naismith refused to name the sport after himself, so it was named "basketball" by one of his students and remains today.

THE BICYCLE

The very first bicycle was presented at the Paris Motor Show in 1818 under the name "draisine", which comes directly from its inventor, namely Karl Drais (full name Karl Friedrich Christian Ludwig Freiherr Drais von Sauerbronn). Drais was a famous German intellectual, and he was an educated man with deep ideals, so much so that he even decided not to use his title of baron and to drop the "von" from his name.

The draisine was like the modern bicycle, equipped with two wheels of which the front one steered but had no pedals or brakes. To get around one had to sit on the saddle and push it with one's feet pointed to the ground. Constructed of iron and wood, Karl Drais presented it at the Paris Motor Show after obtaining some sort of patent. Parisians were enthusiastic about the invention, but the means of locomotion had difficulties and its use spread very slowly among the bourgeoisie of the time.

Pedals were added in the 1860s, giving rise to the velocipede, which had a larger front wheel and to which cranks were added. The wheels at that time were still made of wood; only later were lighter tires introduced. Then in 1869, there was a change from the velocipede to the bicycle invented by Eugene Meyer's High Bicycle. Then in 1884, John Starley invented the safety bicycle that had two wheels of the same size and chain drive, a model that was very successful and became the actual great-grandchild of the present bicycle.

THE SKATEBOARD

The skateboard has no official father, which means we don't know who was the first person that had the idea of experimenting with the madness of running through the streets standing on a small board that resembles a surfboard. It was not passed down to us and it is a direct descendent of surfing, or rather from the world of surfing that spread this tool loved by kids feared by parents (it's always been considered dangerous, but in truth, we have seen far more dangerous things done with a simple bicycle, to tell the truth). It all began in Los Angeles in a store that specialized in surfing gear.

Bill Richard, the owner of the Val Surf Shop, had the idea of offering a non-water activity to his customers, so he signed an agreement with the Chicago Roller Skate Company to have the supply of wheels that were then mounted on the boards. This is how this practice was born and it quickly spread and became wildly popular. At first, it was called "sidewalk surfing" and later on took the name "skateboarding".

THE TELESCOPE

Despite the paternity of the telescope being attributed to the great Galileo Galilei, the name of the inventor of this instrument is, still today, a hot potato. Between the 16th and 17th centuries, it was already represented in the paintings of the Flemish painter Jan Brueghel the Elder, and there is also evidence that there were already some registered patents in Holland in 1608. Sometime later, in 1609, it was Galileo Galilei in person who built his telescope, and he began to observe the celestial vault. It was also Galileo himself who published the "Sidereus Nuncius", the first treaty in which the motions of the moon, Venus, and Jupiter's satellites were described through direct observation. That historical moment can be regarded as the birth of modern astronomy.

THE PONGO

Pongo was born by chance and, most importantly, from a mistake. It was 1952 and it took place in Florence, in a factory that used to produce shoe wax. A dosing error in the chemical formula gave birth to 500 kilos of a very different kind of wax, with a different composition from what the company needed, but above all a wax that had no use for footwear.

When they touched, though, they noticed that the dough was moldable, it didn't soil nor grease, hence the idea of using it for children to play with. It was just a matter of adding a little color, a modeling dough became a game that entertains and educates at the same time.

Before the flood that hit Florence in 1966 and then because of the outbreak of a fire at the plant the following year, they closed the factory and stopped producing it.

MONOPOLY

Do you know how to play Monopoly? We bet you do, and we're pretty sure you force all your family members to sit around the table and immerse themselves in a game during Christmas time so that you can all play the world's most famous board game altogether. We all know it; we have all played with it. But do you know who invented it and when? Its invention dates back to the far 1903 and it was created by Elizabeth Magie, who patented it in 1904 naming it "The Landlord's Game", and then registered it with a second patent in 1924 after making some changes to the original version. Mrs. Magie had conceived the game as a teaching tool to teach the theories of economist Henry George and demonstrate how the system of the time enriched landlords and impoverished tenants. Elizabeth Magie hoped that in the form of a game, it would be more understandable how unfair the system was, and that by having children play it might stimulate an awareness of justice and become more aware. A real educational purpose like this should be behind every game, don't you agree?

THE PLAYSTATION

I can see your eyes lighting up from here! I knew if we talked about this your attention would be suddenly awakened. Well, let's discuss the PlayStation then, the beloved video game console from which children would never want to tear themselves away. When talking about it, though, we can't say it was a discovery: it was an actual invention, made by the Japanese company Sony.

The way of video gaming has been revolutionized by the PlayStation. This console has allowed everyone to play comfortably from home without going to an arcade. It debuted in

1994 and, despite not being the first home console, it was the first one to have good computing power and to provide games with attractive graphics as well as truly cutting-edge features.

The PlayStation became a real icon in the 90s; so much so that they labeled the youngest of that generation as "the PlayStation generation". Sony has released several versions throughout the years, different from the first one and, despite being in the fifth generation, the console keeps on achieving resounding success by beating out the competitors.

This third journey, in which we learned about the inventions that changed our free time and gifted us with many novelties, has come to an end. We could continue the list for much longer, but maybe we will write another book about this topic. How about it?

We're eager to bring you with us while talking about innovations, we'll go in search of those who invented technological objects we all use and that make our lives easier. Are you

ready? Let's take off and learn about technological discoveries.

Before doing so, though, we want to invite you to let us know what you think about what you're reading. Feedback on Amazon could be a great idea. Your opinion matters to us and that's why we would like to hear from you.

TECHNOLOGY. INNOVATIONS AS A WINDOW TO THE WORLD

> *There is true progress only when the advantages of a new technology become for everyone.*
> **(Henry Ford)**

Here we are ready to take a plunge into the world of technology. In this chapter, we want to take you on a journey oscillating between past and future, because – as it is known – technology is progress and it represents the future, but every invention has such a short life that it soon becomes an old idea. There are also technological things, however, that have not only stood the test of time and are passed down to us, but have changed our existence. And we're sure you've at least once wondered who had the brilliant idea of creating such marvels. Are you all set? Off we go, discovering who conceived what...

MP3

Do you know that little instrument that holds so many songs and that you can carry around with you to listen to your favorite music? No, we're not referring to the Walkman, that is another invention, and it predates it. Let's say the walkman is the predecessor of the MP3. The Walkman was launched back in 1979 and it seemed like an incredible innovation. People were actually all convinced that they had the future at their fingertips, or rather their ears, with that little box that allowed you to listen to cassette tapes anywhere, anytime. Just think, by now many people don't even know what cassette tapes are. The MP3 format came along in 1999, a full twenty years later, thanks to two American teenagers, Shawn Fanning and Sean Parker, who decided to put their programming skills to work so that they could enjoy their favorite music in MP3 format (Moving Picture Expert Group-1/2 Audio Layer 3, also known as MPEG-1 Audio Layer III or MPEG-2 Audio Layer III) and by creating the Napster sharing service, an innovative method of listening to music that spread worldwide. The service was, for obvious reasons, shut down after two years (of course, there were many protests and copyright infringement complaints from musicians and recordists) but the phenomenon didn't stop. In those very years, the first portable players for MP3 format appeared on the market. The problem of the materiality of music was dealt with thanks to the algorithm on which this system is based, so since the early 2000s, anyone can carry thousands and thousands of songs with them to listen to anywhere, anytime.

THE USB FLASH DRIVE

Let's talk about another small item that you have surely seen your parents use, the USB flash drive. Do you know that little flash drive that allows you to upload files from your computer? That's the USB flash drive, a very useful gizmo that has replaced the more cumbersome and fragile floppy disks (there has been a remarkable evolution for those as well, but we'll talk about that at another time).

The advantage of the USB flash drive versus the so-called rescue floppy disks is the fact that it has a larger capacity and is much more durable. You certainly can't remember this, but we remember those times when you inadvertently ruined a floppy disk and you could say goodbye to the data on it because it became unreadable. But that is another matter which, fortunately, has now been overcome.

Let's go back to our USB flash drive. The father of this neat invention is Don Morovan, an Israeli entrepreneur, and he filed a patent for it in 1999. Back then, it only had a capacity of 8 MB, and in the December of the following year, it was put on the market by IBM. Morovan has then become very rich by selling the project to a Californian company.

How did he come up with this flash drive? By chance. Years before filing the patent, in 1989, Morovan was in the United States to present to some potential investors a new idea he was developing with his partners. During his presentation, he went on stage and tried to turn on his laptop, but it decided not to work. He was stuck, can you imagine that? As if a teacher called you to the desk to answer a question and your brain was empty and everything you knew was gone suddenly. That must have been terrifying, right? Well, let's go back to Morovan. The man was blocked and his whole presentation was on his laptop, which didn't want to collaborate. And it was at that precise moment that he had a real enlightenment: he should have created a handy support to store data, information, and documents. That support is still used by all of us every day.

3D PRINTING

When we were kids, it was impossible to think about it – it was science fiction! But today, with a simple printer, you can create a three-dimensional object. Can you imagine that now that's what innovation stands for! The idea of 3D printing catapults us directly into the future. But do you know who invented this printing technique and when? Charles Hull, a physical engineer from the USA, created it back in the early 1980s of the 20th century. He worked on it for years, refined this 3D printing technique, and then began selling printers to companies that wanted to make three-dimensional proto-types of their productions. The solution was really good for this purpose because it saved money, employment of people, and time for those who wanted to make a prototype quickly. The use of 3D printing, however, has not stopped at proto-type making. It has expanded to other fields including tech-nology and even medicine. Just think that today even bone components are reproduced with this technique, in a short time and with excellent results. If we then want to peek at what may seem like science fiction, know that studies are be-ing done to be able to look already at the reconstruction of whole organs with organic materials. Can you imagine that? It really looks like living in a science fiction book, doesn't it?

In any case, the use of 3D printing already to date is wide-spread, and it is estimated that in technological develop-ment, that 3D printer will become one of the richest and most powerful markets.

THE E-MAIL

The e-mail has now officially become the substitute for the good old handwritten letters (or for the more avant-garde with a typewriter) and has entered our life as if it was a normal and daily tool. Not everyone knows, though, that this method of exchanging messages from one computer to an-other has existed since the beginning of the 70s, 1971 to be exact, and came into existence by chance thanks to a contract got by the Bolt, Beranek and Newman Company in 1969. The company got the contract to develop the AR-PANET net (which would then become our Internet) and it was during its implementation that an engineer, Ray Tomlinson, did experiments to code two programs, SNDMSG and CPYNET. The first was supposed to allow computers to exchange messages and the second was supposed to make it possible to exchange documents between two computers. Working on this, Tomlinson devised an effective system to be able to make computers belonging to independent networks communicate. His idea to insert the @ symbol (meaning *at*) to separate the username from his net turned out logical. Tomlinson had rescued the commercial "a" from inevitable oblivion (in fact, it is virtually no longer used in other areas today) and created a fast method of communication that would never wane again.

Unfortunately, the engineer did not save the contents of the first email sent because he was not yet aware of the scope of his invention, but he would state that as far as he remembered it could have been a very trivial message such as: TEST 1 2 3 4.

And you know a curious thing? Jerry Burchfiel, Tomlinson's colleague, suggested to Tomlinson that he should not spread the news and keep his discovery a secret because by not falling within the delivery they had given them he would risk an earful from the bosses.

THE MOUSE

Let's talk about another computer-related tool that you know almost surely, and you may have also used it: the mouse. The famous little mouse revolutionized the way of working at the computer and made so many common operations faster. Today you find very little ones but they're so many on the market and some with strange shapes, with lights, without lights, some even no longer need the wire to be connected to the PC. From the moment it was invented, this tool has undergone many evolutions to date. Just imagine that the first mouse was a simple little wooden box equipped with wheels and a very thick electrical cord. Just so you know how much time has passed since that first "little mouse", and have you asked yourself when was it invented and who invented this object which seems irreplaceable to us? The idea came to Douglas Engelbart and Bill English in 1963. The little box should have been part of a wider project that was to help facilitate human-computer interactions. At the time, neither the two inventors nor the Stanford Research Institute for which they worked thought of commercializing the little thing. In fact, years later, the project was taken over and perfected by Xerox Labs, which still failed to popularize the use of the new tool. It had to come to Steve Jobs with Apple in the 1980s to further improve the invention and also make it more reliable, which led to its commercialization. The name "mouse", referred to the animal itself, came from Engelbart precisely because of its shape and the fact that it was attached to the computer by a cable that resembled a mouse's tail.

THE TOUCHSCREEN

Do you know that screen on Mom and Dad's phone that you want to keep touching? Yes, we know it's fun to see that folder open, pictures appear just a touch of your little finger. Touch-screen technology, though, is not a toy, you know that, right? Anyway, scolding you is not our intention. However, you might be curious about how this kind of screen works with the simple touch of your fingers and how it came to be.

Well, the interface based on touch-screen technology dates back to 1971 and is an invention of Samuel C. Hurst.

The idea came to Hurst's mind while facing a problem. He found himself having to enter a considerable amount of data

114

into his computer, a job that would take at least two months to complete-a panic, right? It was at that moment that Hurst decided to create a more practical method of working that would make tasks such as the one he had to perform faster and easier. So, he invented a coordinate measuring system consisting of a sensitive tablet where the data to be combined were located and which recognized where an operator touched with a stylus. Hurst and his staff worked for years perfecting the idea, and in 1977 the first real touch screen was launched, say the ancestor of the touch screen we all have on our phones today.

Did you enjoy traveling in the history of technology? It's always nice finding out where so many technological innovations come from, right? We agree with you: it's always interesting to get to know where ideas originated from and how they developed to come and change our lives. In many cases, as you may have read, the person who had the idea, never suspected the scope their idea would influence nor its lasting effects. Though you have to admit, it's also interesting to find out where even the everyday objects we now take for granted, such as a toothbrush or sneakers, originate, arrive, or are invented. And maybe it would be nice to know how long they have been a part of our lives or, perhaps, if they were discovered by accident or in response to someone's need... Well, in that we can surely accommodate you, follow us in the next chapter where we're going to poke around in history to find out where so many objects that are part of our everyday life came from, to also see by whom and when they were invented or discovered. Are you curious? We're sure your answer is going to be a yes, so let's not wait any longer and run right into the next chapter.

ORDINARY OBJECTS. THEY'RE NOT SO OBVIOUS!

> *To invent, you need a good imagination and a pile of junk.*
> **(Thomas Alva Edison)**

Things you see every day in your house, objects you or your parents use daily, in short, are everyday objects that we now take for granted because we are used to having them on hand. These are the discoveries or inventions we want to talk about in this last chapter. We want to take a tour through history with you one last time to explore when and who invented objects for regular use like the toothbrush or the microwave oven. We already see that you are ready and eager to go on this journey and we certainly don't want to keep you waiting. Follow us as we set off together and dive into the past in search of those who discovered what have now become everyday conveniences for us.

THE SHOPPING CART

You must have gone to the supermarket with your parents a few times. Surely you have helped them with their shopping and insisted on putting the groceries in the cart itself, or you wanted to push it even if it was taller than you. We bet that sometimes, when you were younger, you insisted on getting

116

into that magical metal object with wheels yourself and having your parents push you around the aisles and shelves. We guessed, didn't we? Well, we may be thinking the shopping cart is so old that it always existed. We take for granted that it did. The first cart on wheels was provided by Sylvan Goldman back in 1937. Goldman was a businessman as well as a supermarket owner in Oklahoma, in the U.S.. The man had devised a method to make shopping more efficient and less tiring because he was convinced that in this way customers would be more likely to spend more money in his supermarket. That being said, one day he took a chair, placed a basket in it, and attached wheels to it, creating the first rudimentary shopping cart. You must know that this idea was not as well received as he expected since customers were not inclined to accept such an innovation. There were many reasons why people were not inclined to use the tool, but Goldman didn't give up. He paid models to walk around inside the supermarket pushing his cart and showing how cool it was. And it worked. By 1940, trolleys had become commonplace and almost all supermarkets decided to adopt them.

THE MICROWAVE OVEN

This household appliance is now present in everyone's home and has been used for a long time. Certainly, we must say that the microwave oven has radically changed the way of cooking and made life easier for many people, especially those who had very little time to devote to traditional cooking.

Almost certainly, your parents will also have had to resort to this tool because too many commitments came in their way of enjoying a nice juicy lunch. When they come home from work and have no time to cook dinner, the microwave is the perfect alternative to being at the stove.

Did you know when it was invented, they had no idea it would become a household appliance? Or at least, that it would have been used to cook food? Well, yes, you heard us: microwaves were not meant for cooking but by a twist of fate someone discovered that you could also cook food in them.

It was 1945 and an engineer of Raytheon named Percy Lebaron Spencer was working with magnetrons that emitted microwaves when he noticed that the chocolate in his pocket had melted. Through that experience, he discovered that the microwaves emitted by the magnetron had cooked the bar. That same year Raytheon filed a patent for a microwave cooking process. The household microwave oven was then officially introduced in 1967.

MATCHES

Matches were invented by accident as well, although fire was of common use. It happened in 1826, when an English pharmacist, John Walker, was mixing chemicals containing phosphorus with which he had coated a stick. The man noticed quite accidentally that the stick had a protuberance, and he decided to remove it. He thus set about scraping the stick, causing a spark. He had created the first match without even knowing it. The pharmacist began selling that product, calling it a "friction light", the ancestor of the match. There was one small problem, however, which was the fact that the mixture ignited gave off toxic fumes.

After Walker, two other inventors followed in his footsteps. They were Samuel Jones who called his product "Lucifers" (these matches were also poisonous) and in 1855 the Swede Johan Edward Lundström. The latter patented his own version by separating the phosphorus from the other components, then putting the phosphorus on a strip of sandpaper attached to the box and the rest of the components on the head of the stick. Even in the latter version, however, the fumes given off by the matches were highly toxic. It wouldn't be until 1910 when the Diamond Match Company would finally succeed where all had failed, making a nontoxic match as we know them today.

HEATERS

A great invention, don't you think? Heaters are a really great thing to have in our house, especially during winter. We know you know what we mean when talking about the pleasure of putting our pajamas on after leaving them on the heater before snuggling up on the couch to watch TV with Mom and Dad. It's a real pleasure not only for the youngest but also for us grown-ups who love the warmth the heater gives us on the coldest days, especially when coming back from a hard work day.

Let's admit without shame, the heater is a fabulous and functional invention. But do you know who invented this marvel and when? We're going to tell you right away.

Once there were stoves, before the heater as we know it came about. Stoves, however, were not very functional and very laborious in maintenance because they had to be refilled often with wood or coal. Plus they were unsafe. Heaters, on the other hand, proved to be cheaper but also safer because they use hot water instead of burning the far more dangerous fire.

In 1839, Pietro de Zanna invented and patented the first air heater, but it was not until 1855 when Italian-Russian inventor Franz Karlovich San Galli devised the water heater, which contributed significantly to modern heating systems.

THE TV

And here we are talking about an appliance that we are sure you adore. You like watching television, isn't that so? The TV is also one of those things that you take for granted that has always existed. Instead, we can assure you that there was a time when not only it did not exist, but it was a "devilry" in people's minds.

Of course, we have to go back a long way, back to the distant past but there were long eras when little boys and girls certainly could not watch their favorite animated series or snack in front of a program dedicated just to them like some that are broadcast in the afternoon time slot like now. We can say, though, that the idea of what would become the television we know today is by no means as recent as everyone thinks.

In fact, the first ancestor of television dates as far back as 1883, more than a century ago. A design devised by the German Paul Gottlieb Nipkow and consisted of a rotating circular plate (later called a "Nipkow disk") on which small spiral holes were drilled, which had to be passed through by a light and then interacted with a selenium photocell. This system allowed an image to be scanned and broken down into many regards (which corresponded to the small holes) arranged on different lines. Basically, changes in brightness were translated into electrical pulses and then transmitted and transformed into a light signal, this allowed the image that had been recorded to be reproduced on a screen. I know it sounds very complex to read but it was a simple system and for the time represented a fabulous innovation, as you can well imagine.

At that time there were no means to realize Nipkow's idea concretely, so the project remained as such and never turned into something real. At least that was the case for the next forty years, when in 1925, the Scotsman John Logie Baird took over Nipkow's project and succeeded in shaping the first television system called "electromagnetic", because it was based on a mixture of electronic and mechanical components.

It was Oct. 2, 1925, when Baird arranged in his London laboratory for the first real television broadcast, that is, he beamed his delivery man's face from one room to another.

Of course, the first television image was warped and blurred as well as displaying only grayscale because it could not be in color, but the era of television had begun, and the rest was just a continuing evolution of this appliance now present in every home.

THE EARMUFF

You may have used it some time, maybe during a trip on a snow trip with your parents or while ice skating with your friends. We all have used at least once the earmuff to protect us from the cold. And because of that, we understand why this curious piece of clothing was made, but do we know when and from whom?

This invention comes from the idea of a very young 16-old-boy from Maine, in the USA. It was 1873 when Chester Greenwood decided he had to find a way to protect his ears from the bitter cold when he went skating. The kid turned to his granny, asking her to join two pieces of fur together with a thread so that they could fit over his ears and protect them from the bitter cold that hits Maine in winter. An idea that served its purpose and opened up a path of success for the boy considering that he later founded the Chester Greenwood Company to make to sell his earmuffs.

TOOTHBRUSH AND TOOTHPASTE

You should brush your teeth every time you eat something. And yes, we're talking about the toothbrush and its long-term companion, the toothpaste. We already imagine your parents repeating dozens of times that you have to brush your teeth after eating... and we also imagine you trying to make an excuse and say you'll do it later. That's not how it works! Brushing your teeth is one of the most indispensable and hygienic activities for personal care. Despite this, giving you a hard time trying to convince you to brush your teeth is not our intention. However, you know how we feel about it now.

We're almost sure you have wondered at least once about the inventor of this practice and the origins of both the toothbrush and toothpaste. We're right, aren't we? Well, we're now going to reveal how they came to be, and you'll also realize that this is something not as recent as you might think, it's something that goes back many years ago.

Consider that traces of the existence of the toothbrush have been found three thousand years before the birth of Christ. At that time, a simple twig was used to clean what was chewed, so that as it frayed it cleaned the teeth with a mechanical action. The first toothbrush vaguely like the one we use today was, nonetheless, documented in the 1600s. The spread of this tool, however, came about two centuries later, in the 1800s. The first industrially produced toothbrushes were made in the United States using boar hair, which, as you might guess, contained so many bacteria that instead of exerting a cleaning action they infected the mouth.

Don't make that face! This is no longer the case. It's been many decades now since toothbrushes have been produced with synthetic bristles and are the ultimate in hygiene. There's no excuse not to use them after every meal!

What about toothpaste? Its origins are very distant in time as well. People used to brush their teeth even in prehistoric eras, as you may have seen. And if we go back to the time of the Egyptian Pharaohs (around the 4th century B.C.), they mixed salt, pepper, mint leaves, and iris flowers to make a compound with which they rubbed their teeth. The ancient Romans, on the other hand, compounded human urine to take advantage of its anti-inflammatory properties.

Conventionally, however, the inventor of toothpaste is considered to be Scribonius Largus, a Roman physician in the 1st century A.C., who invented an oral hygiene substance that mixed vinegar and salt (which served as disinfectants) with honey and small glass chips so that the substance became abrasive.

In the 18th century, a toothbrushing paste that was composed of salt, calcium, charcoal, and brick dust was widespread.

If we look at all these mixtures and substances with today's knowledge, we obviously know that they're unsuitable for the purpose. For example, today we know that the use of honey contributes to the formation of tooth decay and not to fighting it, and if we then consider fresh breath, it's certainly not vinegar that comes to our aid. But you know these things too, don't you?

In conclusion, we can say that modern toothpaste, that is, as we know it, made its appearance no earlier than the early 1900s and was already sold in tubes.

TOILET PAPER

We do take toilet paper for granted, don't we? We all use it and, frankly, we would be lost if we realized we ran out of it in case of... need. It used to be a real luxury. Now to talk about its origins: who invented it and when? Well, we're here to satisfy your curiosity. Let's take a brief journey on the history of... toilet paper.

As we were saying, toilet paper in soft rolls — as we know it — was not always available to men (and women, of course). During the primitive era, however, they did their needs as we do, and, go figure, they even had a kind of toilet (primitive of course) that consisted of a hole in the ground or a flat rock. Once they had done their business, men living in the Neolithic period had to find a stream and wash in the water to get rid of the waste. But when it was cold? Perhaps in the frost of winter? How did he clean himself? Not even scholars were able to answer these questions, we can only guess that he resorted to leaves or unsharpened stones (but these are only guesses, really).

Ancient Egyptians, on the other hand, were slightly more organized and used a kind of sand soaked in scented oils, if we think of the Arab and Indian peoples it seems they used their left hand (we know the image is a bit disgusting... however, if you want a curiosity we can tell you that to this day for the Arabs the left hand is considered unclean and it is a serious offense to touch an Arab or to hand him any object with that hand, will there be a connection between the two?).

The real pioneers of intimate hygiene were Asians. We have to go back to the 14th century in China during the empire of Zhu Yuanzhang to see toilet paper appear for the first time. It took several more centuries before even the West abandoned the use of leaves, cloth, or newspaper sheets to wipe one's "back".

In 1558, in Monsignor Della Casa's "Galateo," he talked about some "pezze degli agiamenti" (that is, cloths hung in the lavatories). Even centuries before that time, however, pieces of cloth made from discarded robes were used in convents for cleaning themselves. To get to real use of paper for hygienic purposes as a product, we have to wait until the 1700s. However, that was frowned upon and considered "unmentionable". Just think that at that time ladies kept sheets of toilet paper inside the handle of their fans.

It was in 1850 that New York entrepreneur Joseph C. Gayetty presented his invention, namely, toilet paper as we know it. The public welcomed Gayetty's idea as a great discovery while the medical community accused him of being a quack because Gayetty had named his invention "Medicated paper" and claimed that it had curative power. This obviously did not correspond to reality. In short, medically, it didn't solve any problems, but the paper invented by Gayetty was a huge hit with consumers and began to appear on the shelves of emporiums and supermarkets in the USA.

Paper was sold in packets containing strips of paper that bore the inventor's name and a kind of advertising slogan: "They are as delicate as a banknote and as strong as a sheet of music". Rolls, as we know them today, had to wait until 1879, and two-ply paper (which dissolves more easily in the toilet) came as late as 1942.

There would be so many other items that have become commonplace for us and that we have come to take for granted, but our roundup of discoveries and inventions ends here. Perhaps we will come back later with more discoveries and other curious inventions, but for now, we invite you to follow us to the last chapter, which is the conclusion of this book. But before we move on to the closing, we want to invite you to let us know your opinion of what you have read by leaving us feedback or a comment on Amazon as well. Now, however, let's move on to the conclusion and greetings.

CONCLUSIONS

So, did you enjoy our collection of inventions and discoveries? We are sure your answer is YES!. Writing this book was a lot of fun for us, just as it was fun to go and find out so many things we use every day and which we often underestimate came to be or were discovered.

Wondering when something like the USB flash drive or the school desk was conceived or going in search of the inventor of French fries, not to mention learning how and when someone decided that the earmuff could be a most useful idea in its simplicity, was indeed an exciting adventure. We must say, it's been exciting sharing this research with you and also being able to fill this book with so much useful and informative information – let's think about how the delicious foods you love were created, as well as how items that you use every day in school such as your pencil sharpener or your backpack made our lives easier and, let's not forget, all those everyday objects, those household things that we use every day mistakenly assuming that they have always existed.

Kairoslandd will be back soon with other curious and instructive books like this one. However, in the meantime, we would like to invite you to follow your curiosity from the wonders you have in front of your eyes every single day. We suggest doing as we did when you are faced with an object that you use every day. Ask yourself who invented it, when, and also why, and then go, and look up the information. You will see how fun and exciting it will be to dig into the past and go in search of curious but also useful news. Most importantly, you will realize how much you will learn, all on your own and have a great time.

Sadly, it's time to say goodbye. Ours, however, is not a final parting ways, it is only a goodbye to the next adventure together which, we assure you, will come very soon. In the meantime, continue to study, to be curious, to read, and to have fun, but also (never forget) to be obedient to your parents.

Until the next adventure with Linda and Charlie.

QUIZ

1) In which nation was the first pencil factory created?

a. Sweden
b. Japan
c. USA

2) Pongo was accidentally created by

a. A cream-dough
b. A wax mixture
c. A gummy candy dough

3) The ancestor of the TV dates back to the year

a. 1883
b. 1899
c. 1847

4) Who invented matches?

a. A pharmacist
b. A chemist
c. An arsonist

5) Which technological tool was named after an animal?

a. The one which is used to point objects on the screen.
b. The one which is used to write.
c. The one which is used to print.

6) The Braille alphabet was inspired by

a. Music notes
b. The butterfly alphabet
c. A method of message transmission used by the armed forces

7) John Stith Pemberton's recipe for a headache was then transformed into:

a. An Aspirin
b. Coca Cola
c. A beer

8) What does "draisine" stand for?

a. The first pencil
b. The first bicycle
c. The first pressure cooker

9) The gel pen consists of

a. A gel with color obtained from the distillation of flowers
b. A gel with colors derived from squid ink
c. A gel with water-soluble color pigments

10) Who invented the USB flash drive?

a. Don Morovan
b. Dartagnan
c. Don Caravan

11) Who invented the PlayStation?

a. Sony
b. Nintendo
c. Nvidia

12) What did Mrs. Elizabeth Magie invent?

a. Guess Who?
b. Monopoly
c. Taboo

13) How old was Frank Epperson when he invented the popsicle?

a. 15
b. 11
c. 8

14) What is the so-called "Pascaline"?

a. The first carbonated soft drink
b. The first calculator
c. The first car

15) What did the ancestor of the backpack look like?

a. It was a basket
b. People carried their books by hand
c. It was a wheelbarrow

16) What is the name of the teacher who invented basketball?

a. James Naismith
b. George Baillat
c. Blaise Pascal

17) What is the name of the process that makes rubber durable and usable on paper?

a. Gelling
b. Solidification
c. Vulcanization

18) Who is the father of modern ice cream?

a. Geronimo Maria Pernis
b. Matthew Francis of Pisa
c. Francis Procopius of the Knives

19) In 1937 Ruth Wakefield invented:

a. The chocolate milkshake
b. Chocolate chip cookies
c. Chocolate lollipops

20) What nationality is the most famous lollipop in the world i.e., Chupa Chups?

a. English
b. American
c. Spanish

BIBLIOGRAPHY

Capelvenere Franco, Meucci. *The Man Who Invented the Telephone*, (literal translation from the Italian: "*L'uomo che ha inventato il telefono*"), 2003

Caprara Giovanni, *Brief History of Ggreat Scientific Discoveries*, (literal translation from the Italian: "*Breve storia delle grandi scoperte scientifiche*"), 1998

Challoner Jack, *1001 Inventions That Changed the World*, 2009

Colangelo Giorgio, Temporelli Massimo, *The gang from Via Panisperna. Fermi, Majorana and physicists who changed history*, (literal translation from the Italian: "*La banda di via Panisperna. Fermi, Majorana e i fisici che hanno cambiato la storia*"), 2014

Marchis Vittorio, *The Things of Home. Minimal Chronicles of Domestic Technologies*, (literal translation from the Italian: "*Le cose di casa. Cronache minime di tecnologie domestiche*"), 2014

Morelli Gianni, *The Discoveries and Iinventions That Changed the World From the Late 19th Century to the Present Day*, (literal translation from the Italian: "*Le scoperte e le invenzioni che hanno cambiato il mondo dalla fine del XIX secolo ai giorni nostri*"), 2018

Norton Trevor, *Imagination and a Pile of Junk: A Droll History of Inventors and Inventions*, 2014

Rubino Anthony Jr., *Why Didn't I Think of That?* 2010

Temporelli Massimo, *Innovators. How People Who Change the World Think (Brief History of the Huture)*, (literal translation from the Italian: "*Innovatori. Come pensano le persone che cambiano il mondo (Breve storia del futuro)*"), 2015

KAIROSLANDD

Can you fill the time you spend with your children (Kronos) with joy, beauty, and meaning (Kairos)?

Responsibilities and worries make us forget about ourselves without even noticing that every single second spent away from our loved ones is a second we won't take back.

There's no chance to go back.

Too much time spent between work and commitments without being able to see them grow up, knowing if they're doing fine, missing out on their early discoveries... Learning from TVs and smartphones is what they do nowadays...

We are Linda (elementary school teacher in Florence) and Charlie (Canadian graphic designer), happy parents of two wonderful children and founders of Kairoslandd!

The story you were reading was the story of our lives that was getting out of hand.

Our children were growing so fast, but we knew nothing about them, except what their grandparents told us after spending their days with them.

It sounds strange to hear but a time of world disgrace like the pandemic was a great joy for us. Are you wondering why?!

We enjoyed every minute, laughter, game, and feel of our children as never before, rediscovering how time should be fully lived.

Kairoslandd was born for you, parents and caregivers, who want to be there at the "right time" to fill your mind with unrepeatable memories and emotions so that they will never slip away.

By combining our professional experiences in teaching and graphic design, along with a team of experts, we have created many useful, quality books designed to make every moment you spend with your children magical!

133

SPECIAL QR BONUS

Scan the QR Code with your smartphone camera and let us know what you think:)

ANSWERS

R1: **3**

R2: **2**

R3: **1**

R4: **1**

R5: **1**

R6: **3**

R7: **2**

R8: **2**

R9: **3**

R10: **1,**

R11: **1**

R12: **2**

R13: **2**

R14: **2**

R15: **1**

R16: **1**

R17: **3**

R18: **3**

R19: **2**

R20: **3**

135